EAT
PLAY
LOVE

*The ultimate guide for
every dog owner*

LARA SHANNON

Hardie Grant

TRAVEL

LOVE   165

INTRODUCTION

Growing up I was fortunate to live in front of a river where I spent much of my early childhood out all day exploring and playing with carefree abandon. As an only child, much of my time was spend sharing these adventures with my first dog Rion, a black toy poodle with some serious attitude, who was my confidant. As a teenager it was Tosca, a kelpie cross who was there to help me through the trials and tribulations that come with those awkward, hormone-filled years.

When I left my home town of Adelaide, South Australia to pursue a career in the media and my passion for animal conservation I had to leave Tosca behind. But during those years (when I was out at work all day, socialising at night and living in rental accommodation) I realised that owning a dog would not be fair. Instead I 'adopted' dogs in my neighbourhood whose owners were more than happy to have someone take them for a walk or look after them when they went away without wanting anything more in return than a happy, wagging tail and the canine companionship that I sorely missed.

Max, a cheeky 4-year-old Maltese, came into my life when I returned to Australia in my thirties. He was my four-legged soul mate who saw me through some tough times. Ultimately though, the toughest day of all was when I had to say goodbye as old age and ill health got the better of him. It was because of Max and his separation anxiety and other behavioural quirks that I decided to start working with dogs and become certified in dog training and behaviour.

As my understanding of why dogs do what they do became clearer, I became even more passionate about finding a way to help spread the word about the need to provide our dogs with the training and leadership they need to not just survive, but to thrive in this world.

This led to the creation of Pooches at Play so that I could reach as many people as possible through my TV show and other educational activities.

It also led me to find my next and current furry 'soul mate' Darcy. I was studying dog training and creating a dog show, while minding and training other people's dogs without one of my own when one day this wiry, scruffy little 'bitsa' (bits of this, bits of that) showed up in my life after being given to a friend because he needed a new home.

From the moment we met I just knew he was destined to be part of my life. We forged a bond that was so strong that after a few years of hanging out, walking and minding him at any opportunity I could get, circumstances led to the offer of Darcy officially becoming mine. And, as they say, the rest is history.

With Darcy firmly by my side, we work hard to spread the message about responsible pet ownership, fly the flag for pet adoption and endeavour to communicate to as many people as possible about how to provide the love, enrichment, training and other care dogs needs for a safe, happy and fulfilled life.

Our pets play many important roles in our lives and there are numerous studies from all around the world that support what us dog owners already know – dogs bring us companionship and joy, and their love knows no bounds.

It's no wonder then that they are the most popular pet of choice around the world, with 40% of Australian households, 38% in the US and 25% in the UK owning a dog.

They give us a sense of purpose and improve our physical and mental wellbeing. They reduce loneliness, help rebuild

RION

MAX

TOSCA

trust and connections, and assist many people with mental and physical health issues to live fulfilling, independent lives.

Through this book I hope you will come to understand your dog better and what they need for optimum health. **EAT** aims to unravel the overwhelming options of dog foods available and the things to think about when choosing the right diet for your dog. I also address the concerns and confusion that many dog owners have about today's pet food choices.

As our dogs rely on us to provide them with the mental and physical stimulation they need each day to be healthy and happy, in **PLAY** I talk about the important role of socialisation, training, setting boundaries and being a good leader for your dog to address behavioural issues. I have tried to help explain many of the common issues I see and areas in which many dog owners may still be getting it wrong through no fault of their own, other than a simple lack of awareness and old-fashioned training and behaviour techniques.

LOVE covers topics such as making the decision to become a dog owner, how to choose the right dog for your lifestyle, and how and where to find your next furry friend. I discuss the care you will need to provide through all of the life stages to keep your dog healthy and safe, how to deal with anxiety, multiple dog households and even how to deal with the sad decision you may need to make of saying goodbye. I delve into this and other information and advice to help ensure you are able to provide your dog with the love, care and attention that every dog craves and deserves.

For me this book sums up many of the important messages that I hope every dog owner and dog lover will take the time to read, put into practise and share far and wide, so that together we can ultimately make this a better world for our dogs and for ourselves as a result.

Given all of the unconditional love, devotion and joy they provide to us, it's only fair and right that we return this to our canine companions tenfold.

EAT

WHY FOOD MATTERS

When it comes to choosing the best food for your dog there are so many conflicting messages and options to consider that it can be downright confusing.

Historically, dry dog food (kibble) and canned dog food (wet) were the only commercial choices available to pet owners. However, we are now seeing an ever-expanding number of options as the pet food industry evolves to keep up with consumer trends and a greater focus on pet nutrition. Different food textures, new ingredients and diet types, and a plethora of marketing claims on the packaging (that may not have been substantiated) have made it harder than ever to navigate your way around the shopping aisles.

The best place to start is the ingredients panel on the back of a product to see if it provides a high quality, nutritionally-balanced meal. However, unless you hold a food science degree or specialise in pet nutrition, even looking at the list of ingredients on some products can turn your brain upside down if you aren't sure what exactly you need to look for.

Through my work and pet nutrition studies I know the importance of understanding what you feed your dog. I have also consulted with a wide range of dog food manufacturers, global research reports and industry representatives, independent veterinarians, other pet nutrition experts and other key stakeholders to try to decipher the marketing claims from the actual scientific facts, and everything in between.

For total transparency, I also work with pet food brands through my business, Pooches at Play, and I do have personal views that influence

my food choices for my dog Darcy. However, I have tried to put all of that aside as I take you on my journey to explore the somewhat complex and controversial world of understanding how to choose the right pet food for your dog.

Of course, like us humans, dogs enjoy a tasty treat. So you'll also find some healthy recipes to try at home yourself. (Well, maybe not actually try them in the eating sense ... though some you certainly could ☺.)

JUST TO NOTE, I USE THE PRONOUN 'HE' WHEN REFERENCING A DOG THROUGHOUT FOR CONSISTENCY — NO OFFENCE IS INTENDED TO ALL THE WONDERFUL FEMALE DOGS OUT THERE!

DOG FOOD TRENDS

The impact of millennials

For those of you born between 1981 and 1996, pet food manufacturers know you are a very health and environmentally conscious group and adopt a similar lens to feeding your pets as you do yourselves and your families. In the US, millennials are the largest group of pet owners. As a result, we are seeing this influence new products being brought to the market and driving these key trends as follows:

Transparency – It's very important that brands are authentic, with transparent labelling that clearly represents what is in the food. Manufacturers should be able to demonstrate the science behind their nutritional claims for dogs and not just rely on research done on humans or other animals.

Sustainability – We are now seeing more ethically and sustainably sourced products and practises and more pet owners are prepared to pay more for sustainability over convenience. At the time of writing, in response to finding more sustainable animal protein sources, insect protein was being introduced into feeding trials for cats and dogs. Yes, black soldier fly larvae is now on the menu!

Quality ingredients – Pet owners are increasingly demanding the same qualities in pet food that they want in their own meals; this includes familiar ingredients, sustainability and nutrition. Interest in diets high in protein and fat, with minimal carbohydrates, grains and the use of prebiotics have also been gaining in popularity among pet owners in recent times.

Superfoods – With the rise in human food products containing an array of superfoods, this trend has now spread into pet food, with many including known superfoods such as turmeric, chia seeds, spirulina, kelp, ginger, coconut oil and plant-based proteins.

TREATS WITH THERAPEUTIC BENEFITS

Some pet owners are using treats with cannabis (CBD) as one of the key ingredients to manage pain as well as alleviate stress and anxiety in their dogs. However, the pros and cons of including it in a dog's diet are currently unproven. CBD is also not legally available everywhere.

PET OWNERS IN CHINA

The increase in pet ownership in China has seen emerging trends not found in other countries. Quirky packaging is one; and, like the millennials, pet owners in China will do more research than any other country to establish if they can trust a pet food. Their focus on ingredients has resulted in the inclusion of novel, exotic proteins (freeze-dried quail egg yolks, anyone?) – often represented by large, beautiful photos of the source animals on the pet food packages.

WHAT'S A BALANCED AND NUTRITIONAL DIET?

WHAT SHOULD I FEED MY DOG?

Lots of dog owners ask me this question and despite a multitude of studies and research reports from around the world there is still a lot of conflicting evidence and advice being given about the best diet for dogs. I know how much my mind has boggled studying pet nutrition and trying to take on board all of the opposing views and research. So, let's delve into it together and see what we can find.

How history influenced your dog's diet

Dogs evolved from their wild wolf ancestors at some point between 15,000 and 40,000 years ago. The long process of domestication began to alter both the behaviour and genes of wolves so they eventually became the dogs that we know today. Yet they still share more than 99% of their DNA with wolves.

Although dogs have evolved to thrive on a diet high in animal protein and fat, and low in carbohydrates, they can eat a wide range of foods to survive and are therefore classified as omnivorous carnivores.

In the wild canines obtain the most nutrition from the internal organs of their prey. These organs such as liver, kidneys, heart, spleen and brain are concentrated sources of fat-soluble vitamins such as A, D, E and K. By eating the lining of the digestive system in their prey, dogs obtain a rich source of natural microorganisms including pre and probiotics as well as a small amount of vegetable matter which may be found in the gut of their prey.

Other parts of the prey, including fur, skin and organs such as eyes, are also eaten along with bone, a rich natural source of calcium and phosphorus for teeth and bone health, zinc for immunity and omega-3 essential fatty acids to reduce inflammation. Grasses, fruits and vegetables from their natural environment would also be consumed to stock up on nutrients not found in meat alone, or if a prey source was not available.

How have dogs' diets changed?

Over many generations the metabolism of animals has evolved in response to changes in the food available to them. With domestication, dogs became increasingly dependent on their owners for their food and their diet began to include a wide range of different food scraps, both meat and otherwise.

However, research shows the basis of a dog's diet should still be consistent with the core ingredients and nutrient levels they need. This should include high levels of meat protein, and fat and low levels of carbohydrates in the form of fruit, vegetables and other plant matter, along with bone and other prey matter. Dogs will sometimes eat grass too, which may provide a source of vegetable matter and micronutrients.

Carbohydrates – good or bad?

Carbohydrates are sugars, starches and fibres present in fruit and vegetables, breads and grain products, and sugar and sugary foods. They are used prolifically in many dog foods today as they are a more abundant and cheaper source of calories than meat. Carbohydrates are also needed in the dry food manufacturing process. However, the level of carbohydrates that dogs actually need and should be fed in their

daily diet is often cause for debate and as a result carbohydrate levels in different pet foods will vary significantly.

Research shows that our domesticated dogs can digest and absorb carbohydrates better than their wolfish predecessors. But every dog breaks down starch in different ways so it is definitely not a one-size-fits-all approach.

It's also important to remember that carbohydrates turn into sugars and pet food labels generally do not list carbohydrate or sugar levels. As a result, your dog's food could contain *much* higher levels of sugar than you may realise, which may impact on their health and behaviour, much like ourselves when we have too much sugar in our diet.

If you are unsure about the level of carbohydrates in your dog's diet, seek professional advice.

Dogs don't eat like us

As much as we love them, dogs are not human. Dogs are much less discriminating than us and don't experience cravings or need variety just for the sake of taste the same way that we do. Studies have shown that dogs can identify sweet, sour, salty and bitter tastes, but they only have about one-sixth the number of taste buds that humans do. What drives them more is their sense of smell and individual preferences they may have in relation to aromas, texture, shape and how each individual pooch prefers to chew and swallow its food.

Keeping the diet type format and ingredients the same is key. Any variety or changes you make should be geared towards providing a nutritionally complete and balanced diet. Changes should be slowly phased in to help avoid upsetting their digestive track and stomachs.

I discuss this transitioning process further on pp. 56–57.

Can I mix kibble with raw or wet food?

Mixing dry food in with raw meat or meat organs can impact on the bacteria and gastric acidity levels (pH levels) in your dog's gut. To allow their digestive system to adjust, introduce raw meat slowly (*see* p. 56).

This is why a dog, who is only fed kibble, may not react well to raw bones. Their tummy just can't break it down as well as a dog that eats bones or raw meat regularly.

Does this mean you shouldn't be adding raw or cooked meat to their kibble diet? Not from what I have learned. We know that fresh food is very beneficial to the health of our dogs, but it needs to be slowly introduced so that their gut can start to balance out to a more acidic level.

If a dog is primarily being fed a nutritionally poor dry kibble, then adding some fresh raw or cooked high quality muscle meat, organs and vegetables into their daily meal is highly recommended, or a quality nutritionally balanced canned wet food, to help bolster the level of nutrition the dog is receiving.

When mixing dog food, you need to keep in mind that each serve of a specific diet is designed to provide the full daily nutritional requirements of a dog. So, if you're feeding half of one brand and half of another without taking this into account and striking the right balance, you could risk some nutritional impacts.

IF IN DOUBT
SPEAK TO A
PET NUTRITIONIST

A 2005 study in the *Journal of the American Veterinary Society* supports the benefits of adding fresh ingredients to a dog's diet. This study found that scottish terriers who ate fresh vegetables, particularly green leafy and yellow-orange vegetables, three times per week had a 70%–90% reduced risk of developing bladder cancer, which the breed is prone to. Of course, **vegetables need to be included in the right ratios, and lightly cooked or pulped to aid digestion** (*see* p. 44).

'Just because it says it is premium on the packaging, it doesn't always mean you are getting a better-quality product. That's why it is so important to read the ingredients list and understand the nutritional value the product is really providing.'

Dr Kathy Cornack,
Newcastle Holistic Vet Services

Cheap versus premium dog food

While there are some good foods that cost less, and some expensive foods that don't live up to their price, it's about the quality and quantity of the ingredients. This includes their digestibility and nutritional value meet your dog's individual needs and there is a high level of product quality control. Choosing food on price alone can be misleading.

- Many of the cheaper dog foods available may use lower quality ingredients and a higher proportion of carbohydrates

- You may find you have to feed your dog more of these cheaper products to help him feel full, affecting their weight ... not to mention the quality and quantity of what's coming out the other end

- When you choose a dog food that uses high quality ingredients your dog is generally able to digest more nutrients from less food

- Advantages in choosing a high quality, nutritious diet include better skin and coat, improved behaviour, smaller and firmer stools (less waste in your yard), improved health and much more

- Paying more for a prescription or premium diet doesn't guarantee it is the most nutritional choice

- Purchasing your pet's food from a pet specialty store is a good place to start to get some advice on the range of products and brands available that work to your budget and individual needs

DIET AND YOUR DOG'S HEALTH

There's no doubt that diet impacts on a dog's health in many ways, just as it does for us. In fact, some of the most common problems veterinarians see today are due to a lack of quality nutrition, poor diet and other diet-related conditions.

Does your dog need a review of his diet?

Some things to watch out for:

- Bad breath
- Body odour
- A dull coat
- Dandruff or excessive shedding
- Problematic flatulence
- Diarrhoea or constipation
- Skin allergies
- Weight loss or gain

IF YOU HAVE ANY CONCERNS ABOUT ANY OF THESE, TALK TO YOUR VET

Diet-related diseases

Globally, obesity in dogs is the number one serious disease. It has become such an epidemic I have written a whole section on the dangerous implications of allowing your dog to become overweight on p. 15, but some of the other serious diseases impacted by poor nutrition or over feeding include:

Pancreatitis – Dietary fat is a major cause of pancreatitis, especially for a dog who gets one large helping of fatty food in one sitting. It is something that you should be aware of before it strikes because the warning signs may not always seem that serious, but it is a potentially life-threatening disease.

Diabetes – Diabetes mellitus is the type most often seen in dogs and can be a genetic condition. However, as it is a metabolism disorder it can also be related to improper nutrition and is often triggered by obesity and chronic pancreatitis. Although diabetes cannot be cured, it can be controlled with insulin injections and a strict diet. Speak to your vet if you think your dog may be at risk.

Skin & coat issues – The skin is the largest organ of the body for all animals, and is affected by diet and nutrition. If your dog's diet is lacking essential fatty acids, this can cause a dull, brittle coat and dry, flaky skin. Some dogs can develop food-related allergies causing them to have itchy skin or an unpleasant odour. I will discuss allergies more in other sections (*see* pp. 19 and 193).

Dysbiosis / 'Leaky Gut' Syndrome – If your dog suffers from regular vomiting or diarrhoea, poor gut health may be to blame. Dysbiosis syndrome, often referred to as Leaky Gut can manifest itself in many ways, such as allergies (dermatitis), behavioural problems (hyperactivity), intestinal distress (diarrhoea, gas, vomiting), respiratory issues (asthma), malnourishment and immune system disorders (chronic fatigue, irritable bowel syndrome).

Cancer – Cancer is a disease that is prevalent in dogs and cats, with estimates of one in two to one in three dogs being affected by cancer. While genetics, age, sexual status and environmental factors all play a major role, poor diet is closely linked to an increased cancer risk in our pets, particularly obesity. Fat doesn't just sit on your pet's body harmlessly, it causes inflammation that can promote tumour development, much like it does in ourselves.

POOR NUTRITION OR OVERFEEDING CAN CAUSE SERIOUS DISEASE

Cardiovascular (heart) disease – Nutritional problems can play a major role in heart conditions, although age, genetics and other causes also play a role. Dogs can have issues with heart disease if their diet isn't properly balanced, and one key factor to heart disease in dogs is their sodium (salt) intake. Increased sodium in the diet causes increased levels circulating in the blood which, in turn, can cause water retention in the blood vessels and elevated blood pressure.

THE OBESITY EPIDEMIC

Despite how much we love our canine companions, over 40% of dogs in Australia, close to 50% in the UK and an estimated 53% in the US are considered overweight or obese. So, it seems that many pet owners are either unaware (or in denial) that their dog is overweight, or they don't realise the severity of the health implications that carrying extra weight can have on their dog.

Obesity puts your dog at great risk of other diseases including osteoarthritis, cancer, joint, heart, kidney, liver and pancreatic disease. They will also suffer from greater levels of fatigue, discomfort and reduced mobility, leading to a lower quality of life.

If that isn't enough to make you take a feel of your furry buddy's rib cage to see how they are faring, the following information might:

New research from the University of Liverpool and Mars Petcare's WALTHAM Centre for Pet Nutrition reveals that overweight dogs had a lifespan two-and-a-half years shorter when compared to ideal-weight dogs. When you consider that the average lifespan for a large dog is just 8 years and a small dog 11 years, this is a very sobering fact.

Why our pets are becoming overweight

It can be hard for many people to ignore pleading eyes at the dinner table, not to mention how tough it can be to stop a toddler or children littering the floor with tasty morsels. My mum and dad's dog, Joe, has perfected the beg whenever they have food near, which has earned him some extra kilos and a much slower gait, which I noticed on my last visit home. Needless to say, a daughter-to-parent lecture ensued and a strict diet regime was implemented, so I know first-hand how hard it can be for owners not to cave in.

The most common causes of the obesity epidemic in dogs are an improper diet and/or an insufficient amount of exercise. However, as I explained to my parents, what might seem like just a tiny bit to us adds up throughout the day and you could actually be feeding the equivalent of a whole extra meal for your pet without even realising! It is estimated that feeding your dog one little cookie, for example, is the equivalent of the average-size woman eating an entire hamburger!

DOG TREAT TRANSLATOR

Too many unhealthy snacks can add up fast! A cookie or a piece of cheese may seem like a little treat, but it's a whole meal for dogs.

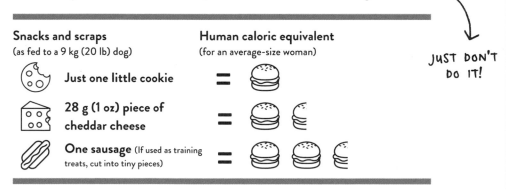

Snacks and scraps
(as fed to a 9 kg (20 lb) dog)

Human caloric equivalent
(for an average-size woman)

Just one little cookie =

28 g (1 oz) piece of cheddar cheese =

One sausage (If used as training treats, cut into tiny pieces) =

JUST DON'T DO IT!

[Source: hillspet.com/pet-care/nutrition-feeding/human-food-treat-translator]

SLOW AND STEADY WEIGHT-LOSS IS KEY

IS YOUR PET OVERWEIGHT?

Your vet is the best person to assess your pet's weight. As there is a large natural variation between breeds of dogs and cats, they use a Body Condition Score, as well as actual body weight to assess them.

If you need some help at home on determining what your dog's ribs should feel like, The Knuckle Test can help.

The Knuckle Test

Do you have a furry or hairy pet and can't see their body shape to tell if they're at a healthy weight? Use this simple test instead.

 **1** Lightly run your fingers over your knuckles as you make a fist. If you imagine those knuckles were your dog or cat's ribs, that would be too thin.

 **2** Put your palm up, fingers extended facing the ceiling. Run your fingers over the base of your fingers – if this were your pets ribs, this it too heavy.

 **3** Turn your hand over, palm down and feel over your knuckles. When your pet's ribs feel like this, it's just right – healthy, lean pet body condition!

BIG DOG PET FOODS

Slow and steady is the key

You may think that simply feeding your dog less will make him slim down, but it is important that you do talk to your vet so that they can help you work out a slow and steady weight-loss plan without jeopardising your dog's health.

Take a closer look at the type of pet food your dog is eating so you can ensure your dog is getting all of the essential proteins and nutrients they need, without the high-calorie fillers or a high-fat content. This is especially important if your dog has a slow metabolism or is not getting enough exercise.

Weigh him every 3–4 weeks and keep a record of the weight. Regular weigh-ins, regardless of whether your dog is overweight or not, can help you keep track of any movement in your dog's weight.

FOOD ALLERGIES

Banfield's *State of Pet Health Report* for 2018 found that only 0.2% of the 3 million dogs and cats in their care actually suffered from food allergies.* The most common causes of allergies included flea allergies and environmental allergens such as dust, pollen and mould spores.

It isn't an easy process to identify a food intolerance or allergy as dog foods are made with a wide variety of ingredients and there is a broad range of things that could be the cause, including a genetic predisposition. The most common dog food allergies and intolerances are to the meat proteins such as beef, chicken, lamb, pork and fish, as well as dairy, soy, wheat and corn.

Getting professional assistance is essential as it takes time and dedication to determine the cause of an allergy. A food trial needs to continue for at least eight weeks and your dog needs to eat nothing that it normally eats before the trial's success or failure can be evaluated.

Regardless of which way you go, if you find your dog is not reacting to the alternative diet they are being fed, then stick with their new diet, and be sure that the manufacturer has processes in place to ensure there is no risk of cross contamination with other proteins or ingredients that are not listed on the label.

* The results are based on data for the preceding 12-month period and only for the pets whose data was included in the study.

'If your vet says your dog needs to be eating a prescription diet due to allergy concerns, ask them to review the ingredient list with you and explain their reasoning for advising the prescription diet, including the specific use of those ingredients. It is often possible with expert advice to formulate an alternative, more natural diet, that can serve the same purpose as a recommended prescription diet.'

Dr Kathy Cornack, Newcastle Holistic Vets.

HOW IS DOG FOOD REGULATED?

Pet food standards

DEPENDS
ON YOUR
COUNTRY!

The pet food regulations or standards are guidelines for the minimum and/or maximum levels of particular ingredients which should be included in pet food for optimal nutrition. They also regulate the claims pet food companies can make about their products.

There is no universal standard for the production of pet food worldwide. In some countries, the manufacturing and marketing (labelling and advertising) of pet food is regulated by national governments or government agencies, self-regulated standards set by industry associations or, in the case of Europe, by various European Union-wide regulations that are upheld by the governments in each country.

The National Research Council (NRC) of the US National Academy of Sciences is the leading provider of nutrient recommendations for dogs and cats. These recommendations form the basis for the Association of American Feed Control Official's (AAFCO) nutrient profiles. They have become the foundation for most state laws and regulations in the US. It is the Food and Drug Administration (FDA) that is responsible for regulating the manufacturing of pet foods as well as determining general labelling requirements for food packaging in the US.

FEDIAF is the trade body representing the European pet food industry and the European Union (EU) regulations rely in part on recommendations from the NRC. The EU regulations are often considered to be the most robust, as they encompass ingredients and ingredient sourcing, as well as manufacturing facilities' hygiene, equipment and environmental impacts. They are also enforced by the law. At the time of printing, the UK hadn't formally separated from the EU, so the UK pet food industry may have their own regulatory body once the formal exit from the EU is complete.

Japan, Singapore and New Zealand also have enforceable pet food regulations, while Canada has a largely voluntary system, as does Australia. At the time of writing, the Australian Standard for the Manufacturing and Marketing of Pet Food is a voluntary standard applied through the Pet Food Industry Association of Australia (PFIAA) and bases its recommendations on the AAFCO nutrient profiles. However, public outcry following the recall of a dog food brand linked to a cluster of related dog deaths highlighted the inadequacies of the voluntary system, with a federal Senate inquiry report calling for the introduction of compulsory rules.

DECODING PET FOOD LABELS

To help you better understand dog food labels, here is a summary of the key information you should pay attention to, noting that it may vary slightly depending on the regulatory system in place in your country of residence.

Identification as a dog food – Pretty self-explanatory, not designed for humans … or cats! There are some distinct differences between a cat and dog's nutritional needs, which is why it is important to feed your pet species-appropriate diets only.

Nutritional adequacy statement – the nutrition claim – A dog food diet must have adequate levels of the nutrients dogs need to survive and are formulated for these specific nutrients, rather than specific ingredients. The nutrition claim is a statement that indicates the food is complete and balanced for a particular life stage of a dog. For example, if a dog food claims to be specifically designed for puppies, it should have the correct nutrients, at the right levels needed by puppies.

Variety and namers – The variety name of a pet food should provide an informative description of the style and flavour. For example, a product may be called 'beef' where beef is the main meat ingredient and is present at more than 25%*. However, this is one reason why **it is really important to read the full ingredients list** to see what else is included, especially if your dog has sensitivities to other meat proteins

* *AAFCO standards. This minimum per cent may differ depending on the standards for the specific country the product is manufactured and/or sold in.*

or ingredients, as a beef variety may well also contain chicken, fish or other meat proteins at lower levels. These *should* be listed further down in the ingredients list.

Best before date – Pet food labels with a longer shelf life (2 years or more) should include a packaging date. In the case of shorter shelf life products, such as fresh or frozen meals that require refrigeration, labelling will include either a best before statement or a use-by-date.

Feeding guide – The feeding instructions are there for a reason, as the nutritional values and benefits listed on the product are based on these instructions. Remember they are a **guide only** based on a recommended daily calorie intake for a dog that is in their healthy weight range.

EXAMPLE OF A RECOMMENDED DAILY FEEDING CHART

Up to 2.5 kg (5 lb)	¼–½ cup
2.6–4.5 kg (6–10 lb)	½–¾ cup
4.6–7 kg (11–15 lb)	¾–1 cup
7.1–9 kg (16–20 lb)	1–1¼ cups
9.1–11 kg (21–25 lb)	1¼–1½ cups
11.1–13.5 kg (26–30 lb)	1½–1¾ cups

GUARANTEED OR TYPICAL ANALYSIS STATEMENT

The Guaranteed Analysis (GA) is a chart usually found on the back or sides of pet food packaging and provides information regarding the four nutrients: protein, fat, fibre and moisture. These are the crude measurements of the content and don't indicate quality or digestibility. Other nutrients are sometimes listed such as calcium, phosphorus, zinc and other vitamins and minerals, or the mineral content may simply be listed as crude ash (which is all that would be left if the product was incinerated).

GUARANTEED ANALYSIS

Crude Protein (min.)	32%
Crude Fat (min.)	14%
Crude Fiber (max.)	5%
Moisture (max.)	10%
Docosahexaenoic Acid (DHA) (min.)	0.05%
Calcium (min.)	1.2%
Phosphorus (min.)	1%
Zinc (min.)	140 mg/kg
Selenium (min.)	0.35 mg/kg
Vitamin E (min.)	150 IU/kg
Omega-6 Fatty Acids* (min.)	2.5%
Omega-3 Fatty Acids* (min.)	1%
Glucosamine* (min.)	600 mg/kg
Chondroitin Sulfate* (min.)	500 mg/kg

*Not recognized as an essential nutrient by the AAFCO Dog Food Nutrient Profiles

The GA can be useful if you want to compare two products. However, it can cause confusion when you are comparing different formats as the tables list the percentages on an as-fed basis. A meaningful comparison can be made by removing the moisture content, so that you are comparing the dry matter only. It is actually quite simple to do once you know how it works.

EXAMPLE OF HOW TO COMPARE THE MINIMUM PROTEIN IN TWO DIFFERENT PET FOODS

Dog Food	Guaranteed Analysis Protein	Guaranteed Analysis Fat	Guaranteed Analysis Moisture
Wet Chicken Recipe	8.5%	5.5%	78%
Dry Chicken Recipe	24%	14%	10%

Look at the canned wet food product example in the above table. The guaranteed analysis lists 8.5% minimum protein, 5.5% minimum fat and 78% max moisture. Whereas the dry kibble lists 24% minimum protein, 14% minimum fat and 10% max moisture.

To make a direct comparison of the minimum protein levels in the two products we would make the following calculations:

Canned wet example	Dry food example
Step 1 Begin by subtracting the moisture percentage from 100	
100 - 78 = 22	100 - 10 = 90
Step 2 Divide the protein percentage by the number you calculated in step 1	
8.5 divided by 22 = 0.386	24 divided by 90 = 0.266
Step 3 To make this a percentage, multiply the answer in step 2 by 100	
0.386 x 100 = 38.6% of minimum protein.	0.266 x 100 = 26.6% of minimum protein

This calculation shows that the canned wet food actually has 38.6% minimum protein and the dry food only 26.6%. You can use the same calculations to compare fat levels.

The percentage of carbohydrates are often not listed on labels, so to calculate the percentage of carbohydrates in a commercial diet, subtract the percentages of protein, fat, moisture, fibre and ash from 100. This can also help you identify how much sugar is really in your dog's food as well, as carbohydrates turn into sugars, which again is not something listed on the ingredients label.

Just remember that the labels are guaranteed minimums and maximums, *not the actual amounts*. So, if your dog needs a low-fat diet, you'll need to make sure you look at the total calories and look for products that are lower in calories when compared to similar foods.

Ingredients list

The most important information on the packaging, in my opinion, is the ingredients list. Most, if not all, of the regulations or standards require pet food labels to list the ingredients (with the exception of water) in descending order (by weight), much the same as our human food. Working off the AAFCO standards, it should also provide information about what species of animal meats (e.g. poultry, beef, fish) are in the product along with food additives, including flavours, colours, preservatives, vitamins and minerals.

WHAT TO LOOK FOR

Assuming your dog is a healthy adult dog with no special considerations, the following is a list of what I consider to be the most important things to look out for and what I take into account for my own dog, Darcy. I've also clarified some of my own concerns and questions with pet health and nutrition experts and have compiled this list that I think most would agree on (and trust me, that is not an easy consensus to get!).

PROTEIN IS #1

1. Protein (ideally from meat) should top the list – If the first five ingredients contain at least three meat sources, you're in good shape – well your dog should be at least!

Proteins are made up of 20 amino acids and, while dogs can produce about half of the amino acids on their own (as long as their diet contains enough nitrogen), there are 10 amino acids that must be supplied by their food and are termed essential amino acids.

Protein from real meat is generally the highest quality and the least processed form of protein. Look for a named meat (chicken, beef, lamb and fish) within the first three ingredients on the list.

Many of the higher quality products will specifically list the main muscle meat product as the first ingredient i.e. chicken, with the individual by-products i.e. chicken liver, chicken heart, ground chicken bones etc. also listed high up on the ingredients list for greater transparency.

2. Fats – Fats provide energy, as well as taste and flavour and they facilitate the absorption of vitamins A, E, D and K. They are made up of fatty acids and, like protein's essential amino acids, there are certain ones that dogs need in their diet because the body cannot make them. They are known as essential fatty acids. They will also help your dog maintain healthy skin and a shiny, healthy coat. While the NRC provides a guide of at least 5.5% fat and 10% protein, 10%–15% fat and 18%–25% protein is a common recommendation for normal, healthy adult animals. This will differ for different life stages or for under or overweight dogs, so talk to your vet about the individual levels they recommend for your dog.

3. Grains, legumes, fruit and vegetables – When looking at the list of ingredients in your dog's food, you might see grains such as barley, corn, oats, rice, wheat, rye and sorghum included for energy, fibre, vitamins and minerals. Whole grains are unprocessed and tend to be viewed as healthier because their nutrients are not degraded by processing.

There can be differing opinions on how much carbohydrate should make up a dog's diet and whether or not grains should be included (*see* p. 7 for more information).

We are also seeing an increased use of legumes and other plant-based protein sources including soybeans and green peas to replace animal proteins as a cheaper and/or more sustainable alternative. It's important to note that plant protein alone does not supply those essential amino acids dogs need in their daily diet, so you are likely to find that synthetic essential amino acids, vitamins and minerals have been added where there is not enough quality meat product to supply the required amounts.

PRESERVATIVES AND ADDITIVES EXPLAINED

Some additives serve an important purpose: nutritional additives improve the nutritional value of the diet, emulsifiers and stabilisers prevent different ingredients from separating, sensory additives can enhance digestibility or even flavour of the ingredients, and preservatives are added in order to extend the shelf-life of a product.

Chemical additives such as preservatives and colourings can become problematic for some dogs.

Vitamins – Fresh, wholesome food provides your dog with the best source of vitamins and organic substances required for normal functioning of their body. Where they may not be naturally present, dog food manufacturers will add vitamins in the form of liquid and powder to ensure they are meeting the requirements for a specific balanced diet. Vitamins C and E are antioxidants and can also act as a natural preservative. The B vitamins are included in most dog foods, while vitamins A, D and K may be added. There are some concerns about the absorption and accumulation of synthetic vitamins and minerals in your dog's tissues forming toxicity instead of being naturally excreted like natural vitamins. This is particularly a concern with the fat-soluble synthetic vitamins A, D, E and K.

Minerals – Minerals are inorganic nutrients that make up less than one per cent of a dog's body weight but are essential to many important functions, such as growth, and strong bones and teeth. Sodium, calcium, zinc and phosphorus are the minerals most often added to dog food. Getting the right balance is critical with all minerals because they interact; too much of one can interfere with the absorption of another.

Pre and probiotics – Prebiotics, probiotics and enzymes can be added to dog food. Depending on the format and quality of the diet you feed your dog, there may already be enough of these naturally occurring to avoid

them having to be added. You may see a reference to these as naturally occurring or added.

Food colours and dyes – These may alter smell, appearance, taste or texture of the food respectively. Food colours and dyes are often added to commercially manufactured pet food in the form of iron oxide or titanium dioxide. Natural flavours may also be extracted from poultry or fish and added to a dog food, or synthesised imitations of similar flavours may be added.

Salt – Salt (sodium chloride) is another common additive that can be found in high levels in some pet foods. It is used to make food taste good and as a preservative. Animals require a certain amount of salt within their diet, but an excess of this can diminish the potassium levels within the body. Table salt is commonly used whilst other salts, which may be used as a preservative, are chloride, nitrates, nitrites and phosphates. Too much salt in your dog's diet can impact on kidney and heart disease so it should be carefully monitored.

Sugar – Sugar, like salt, has also been used as a preservative for centuries and was one of the first substances used. It is argued that there is no need to add sugar as a preservative to pet food and that it can cause long term health problems such as hyperglycaemia, obesity, tooth decay and allergies. Sugar from carbohydrates will not be listed on the label so you won't know the true levels of sugar in your dog's food, which is why doing the GA calculations can help (*see* p. 26).

NO EXTRA
SWEETNESS
REQUIRED

Synthetic antioxidants – Synthetic antioxidants are artificial preservatives which help to prevent food spoilage. Some examples of synthetic antioxidants include butylated hydroxyanisole (BHA), butylated hydroxytoluene (BHT), tert-butyl hydroquinone (TBHQ), ethoxyquin and propyl gallate which are all included in a variety of pet foods. There has been advice to dog owners in particular to avoid synthetic antioxidants, and to only use foods with natural antioxidants, such as ascorbic acid (vitamin C) and tocopherols (vitamin E).

Sulphites – It is known that sulphite preservatives in pet food can cause deficiency of the essential nutrient thiamine (vitamin B1) from food, which causes severe neurological symptoms and can be fatal. The names and numbers to look for are sulphur dioxide 220, sodium sulphite 221, sodium bisulphite 222, sodium metabisulphite 223, potassium metabisulphite 224, potassium sulphite 225 and potassium bisulphite 228.

Chelating agents – These are chemicals added to foods in order to bind metal ions such as iron, cobalt and copper, and are widely used in animal foods. Ethylenediaminetetraacetic acid (EDTA) is a chelating agent used in pet foods. EDTA is labelled safe for health in the quantities used in foods.

Emulsifiers and Stabilisers – Lecithin (E322) is a widely used emulsifier in both human and animal food. It is usually extracted from either egg yolk or soy beans. Common stabilisers that are used in animal foods include: alginate, gelatine, pectin and xanthan gum. Carrageen is another stabiliser used which some specialists argue may pose health risks to the digestive tract.

HOW NATURAL IS 'ALL NATURAL'?

It can often be hard to discern what's true from what's just tricky lingo. The extent of the marketing claims a company can make on their pet-food packaging will vary in every country due to different rules and regulations. Terms like 'contains natural ingredients' may mean there is a little bit of a natural-occurring ingredient in the food, but it may not be much.

Naturally sourced/harvested or occurring may mean that an ingredient was naturally sourced once upon a time, but since then the ingredient may have gone through processing, so therefore isn't actually in a natural state anymore.

If you are truly wanting as close to natural product as you can get, the best thing to do is see how much of the ingredients list looks like real food – do they clearly state they are 100% natural and contain no synthetic ingredients such as added vitamins, minerals and preservatives?

Foods with low quality or plant-based proteins may be missing some of the essential amino acids found in meat, so they'll have to be added back in as synthetic amino acids. You might see them listed as DL-Methionine, L-Lysine, Taurine or L-Carnitine.

Ideally, you want your dog to get real amino acids from his food, not fake ones made in a lab, so look for a simple and clear ingredients list with real food products listed, rather than a long list of words that look like they belong in a science lab.

IF ALL ELSE FAILS, CALL THE COMPANY

While no pet food company will give you their exact recipes for their food, you should be able to get the following information to make an informed decision:

- Protein, fat and carbohydrate content of their food

- What are the natural versus synthetic vitamins and minerals used?

- What preservatives or preservation methods do they use to keep their food fresh and how does this impact on the nutritional values or a dog's health?

- What are the ingredients that you don't recognise? They should be able to talk you through this and explain why they are in their food

- Where do they source their meat and other ingredients from?

LABELS – WHAT TO LOOK FOR

- ☐ Scientifically formulated to provide a complete and balanced diet and/or display certifications such as AAFCO (US), PFIAA (AUS) or FEDIAF (EU)

- ☐ Use high-quality named animal proteins i.e. beef, chicken etc. as the first ingredient, and ideally appear more than once in the first few ingredients, rather than a generic meat meal or plant-based protein

- ☐ Contain natural preservatives rather than synthetic preservatives and additives

- ☐ Use whole grains which contain the entire grain kernel rather than refined grain products

- ☐ Contain some fruit and vegetables

- ☐ Ingredients are tested for contamination before they are used

- ☐ The manufacturer is transparent and willing to answer your questions

- ☐ Have strict manufacturing safety procedures in place to reduce cross contamination (particularly important if your dog has a known food intolerance or sensitivity)

- ☐ Can support any claims appearing upon the label relating to particular product benefits

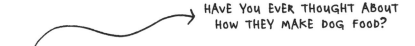

HAVE YOU EVER THOUGHT ABOUT HOW THEY MAKE DOG FOOD?

DOG FOOD TYPES EXPLAINED

When I talk about dog food type, think about it in terms of the texture, shape, size and even flavour of the food. Which format to feed your dog comes down to their individual needs and preferences, i.e. some dogs may enjoy chewing away on crunchy dry pieces of kibble, while others prefer or need a soft, aromatic, wet texture. It is also influenced by owner preferences when it comes to the handling or storage of dog food, budget, or even what the breeder or vet has recommended.

THE FORMAT YOU CHOOSE MUST HAVE ALL THE NUTRIENTS REQUIRED FOR A COMPLETE AND BALANCED MEAL

Dry dog food (kibble)

Dry dog food, also known as kibble, is the most common form of pet food on the market. Available at virtually any price point, the two biggest drawcards of dry dog food are price and convenience. Food can be left out for longer periods than wet or raw food without spoiling and it stores well, so it can be purchased in bulk to reduce cost.

Kibble's primary distinction is its production process and how that process affects its shelf life. Kibble goes through an extrusion process where large batches of the ingredients are mixed and pulverised in order to make a consistent dough that is then cooked under extremely high pressure and temperatures. That mixture is then extruded or pressed through a machine, and cut into individual pieces before being dried to lower the moisture content to 8%–12%. Some dry pet food and treats are made through a baking process where the dough will be cut into specific shapes and baked in an oven.

Carbohydrates typically make up anywhere from 30%–70% of a dry dog food. They come mainly from plants and grains, providing energy in the form of sugar and giving the dry kibble its structure and texture. The most common types of carbohydrates used in dog foods are cereal grains including barley, oats, rice, wheat, corn and millet. Common carbohydrate sources will usually be listed in the first few ingredients on the bag and even if a kibble is grain free it will still contain high levels of carbohydrates, as some sort of starch is required to hold the meat and fat together to form the kibble. Common grain free sources include potatoes, sweet potatoes, lentils, peas, beans or chickpeas.

Once transformed into kibble, many of the nutrients, vitamins and minerals will have been lost in the extrusion process. This includes those essential amino acids, so synthetic versions such as taurine will be added back in, along with the other synthetic vitamins and minerals to help the product meet the minimum nutritional requirements set out under the AAFCO, FEDIAF or other recommendations.

Many dry pet foods also include synthetic preservatives ethoxyquin, BHA, and BHT to help prevent spoilage and prevent fats and oils from becoming rancid. They also contain stabilisers, gelling agents and palatability enhancers such as yeast, fat, sweeteners or concentrated flavours.

When looking for a higher quality dry food product, it is often suggested to look for those that use a single

THE PROS

- Longer shelf life
- Convenient / easy storage
- Less risk of bacteria or spoilage if left out
- Cost effectiveness
- Can be used easily as a training treat and for enrichment games, toys and puzzles
- Can be used with a timed or remote automatic feeding device for dog parents who may not be home by the usual feeding time

source of real meat or fish as the primary ingredient, carbohydrates from vegetables or quality whole grains (unless your vet has recommended grain free for specific health issues), natural preservatives such as rosemary extract or tocopherols (a form of vitamin E) instead of synthetic ones and 100% natural flavours wherever possible.

TIPS IF FEEDING KIBBLE

🐾 Try to add some fresh meat and organ protein to your dog's diet to lower the glycaemic load and replace some of the missing natural vitamins and minerals

🐾 If adding raw or canned wet food to a kibble diet, remember to reduce the kibble intake accordingly to avoid overfeeding

🐾 Look for real meat or fish as the primary ingredient

🐾 Keep in resealable bag/airtight container

🐾 Feed by the best before date

🐾 Keep away from light & heat

DON'T FORGET TO FILL UP THEIR WATER TOO

THINGS TO THINK ABOUT

- Kibble is low in moisture. It's more important to be aware of this as an animal ages, when an animal is ill, in dry, hot climates or with limited access to water

- Easy to overfeed dogs with kibble, as it is so heavily dehydrated

- High carbohydrate levels which may impact on digestibility depending on the dog's ability to breakdown starches

- Lower-quality brands may use only meat by-product or meal instead of real meat

- High use of preservatives, synthetic vitamins and minerals and other additives may lead to dry, itchy skin and irritations

- There is still a risk of accidental contamination in dry food, as highlighted by recalls in recent years

Wet dog food

Wet foods include both canned foods and food in foil trays and pouches.

Wet foods have a much higher moisture content than kibble, usually around 70%-80%, and canned food usually has a much higher percentage of protein than dry dog food. Canned foods can vary in quality too, so you need to check the Guaranteed or Typical Analysis and ingredients list to compare quality and quantity (*see* p. 26 on how to do this).

The type and quality of meat being used may vary, with more meat by-products than muscle meat being included. Don't forget though that even if we humans are put off by some of the parts used such as the kidney, heart, liver, stomach and intestine, this offal is rich in the vitamins and minerals that dogs need.

Wet foods are also often higher in fat, but they don't require the higher amounts of starch that kibble does. They use ingredients such as guar gum or cassia gum (natural thickening agents) to provide the food with some texture, form and shape. Canned food may use other thickening agents such as wheat flour, rice or other grains in addition to minerals and vitamins that have been lost during the heating process.

Unlike dry foods, less preservative is added to wet foods which means the sterilisation process,

THE PROS

- Increases a pet's daily water intake and improves overall hydration
- Aromatic and palatable, so can appeal to fussy eaters
- Can be a good choice for senior or sick dogs who are losing their sense of smell or lacking in appetite
- Easier to determine portion sizes, less carbs, more water for overweight dogs
- Good for dogs that are missing teeth, poorly aligned jaws or smaller mouths
- Has a long shelf life without the need for synthetic preservatives
- Convenient to store
- Can provide additional nutrients and taste if used as a topper to kibble

involving heat and pressure sealing, is extremely important for shelf life.

The higher protein and fat content, as well as the real-food taste, help explain why these wet foods appeal to dogs so much. So, as always, read the ingredients list to try to determine the quality of the product you are choosing.

TIPS IF FEEDING WET/CANNED FOOD

🐾 Use by the best before date

🐾 Once open, cover/seal unused portions, refrigerate and use within 3 days

🐾 Add a quality wet food as a topper to a dry food diet to increase nutrient levels and palatability

🐾 If adding to a kibble diet, understand calorie levels of both diets and reduce the kibble servings accordingly to avoid overfeeding

THINGS TO THINK ABOUT

- Check real meat protein, fat levels and any grains added, as this can vary by quality
- Depending on quality, wet food can be more expensive than kibble
- Can spoil quickly
- Can still be prone to contamination
- An all wet diet can cause loose stools in some dogs
- Some high meat protein pet food in pouches may be a supplement rather than a nutritionally balanced core diet
- Pouches may have higher levels of salt and sugar than canned

> ## MYTH-BUSTER: DENTAL CARE
>
> A common misconception amongst dog owners is that feeding dry kibble will clean your dog's teeth. Some pet food companies do produce an oral care kibble range with a texture, size and shape which they state helps wipe away plaque from the surface of the tooth. Those that I have investigated further still note however, that if tartar is already present, the only way to remove it is with a professional clean by a veterinarian, and that regular dental check-ups and professional cleans are the only way to keep dental disease at bay.

Raw-food diets (BARF and RMBD)

The BARF (Biologically Appropriate Raw Food or Bones and Raw Food) diet is based on what wolves and canines would eat in the wild. Essentially it is all about feeding dogs species-appropriate food that their physiology is best able to digest, including a diet high in animal protein and fat, and low levels of carbohydrates. In the wild, wolves and wild dogs would eat all of their prey (muscle, organs and bones) as well as fish, eggs and some vegetation. Fortunately there are a growing number of scientifically formulated BARF diets to help remove the effort and risk of nutritional deficiences.

I can tell you from my own experience that trying to do it yourself is not easy and you may be putting your dog at risk of tummy upsets or worse, nutritional deficiencies. If Darcy could talk (well he does to me in a language I understand ... but that's a whole other book!) he would tell you that my DIY raw-food diet was a complete disaster! Thank goodness I took heed of the warning signs (stomach gurgling, a loss of energy and enthusiasm for play, not to mention his reduced interest in food and some

GET SOME
SPECIALIST ADVICE
BEFORE MOVING
TO A BARF OR
RMBD DIET

very unpleasant messages via his back end) and put him on to a high quality, Australian-made (remember, he and I are Aussies), commercial raw-food diet which he now thrives on.

To make up your own blend of raw food diets for your dog at home make sure you understand the variety of ingredients and at what levels, so the food supplies the full range of nutrients that your dog needs in its diet. If you get it wrong it can lead to deficiencies or over-representation of different vitamins, minerals and nutrients that can negatively impact on your dog's wellbeing, like it did with Darcy. While you might think you are doing the right thing for your dog by lovingly making their meal at home, you may in fact be doing more harm than good. This goes for both raw and cooked homemade meals. An example of a raw food recipe can be found on p. 46.

The Raw Meat Based Diet (RMBD) or the Whole Prey Diet is similar to the BARF diet, but no vegetables or grains are included at all. The concern around all meat whole-prey dog diets is that they can vary widely in ingredient and nutrient composition and there is a risk of not providing the delicate balance of micro and macronutrients that a dog needs for a complete and balanced diet.

There are some concerns about the pathogens found in raw meat, as they can pose a risk for anyone, dog or human, who has a compromised immune system. However a healthy dog's digestive system is highly acidic which will neutralise bacteria.

WASH YOUR
HANDS AND
UTENSILS AFTER
HANDLING
DOG FOOD

On this, if you are moving to a raw food diet, it is important that you slowly introduce raw food into your dog's diet, particularly if they have been on a kibble diet only, to allow their gut to reach a more acidic state so they can efficiently digest the raw meat and bone. There is more on moving to a new diet on pp. 56–57.

THE PROS

- Ingredients remain nutritionally dense and high quality as they are not adversely affected by cooking
- If prepared correctly, no need for the addition of synthetic vitamins and minerals
- Depending on the country you reside in, high quality, commercial raw-food diets are now readily available from pet specialty stores, taking the hard work out of preparing a raw food diet
- Reduced stool volume and odour
- Improved skin condition and softer, shinier coats*
- Reduced body odour*
- Dental benefits where raw, safe and appropriate-sized bones are given 1–2 times a week (*see* pp. 70–72 for bone safety tips)
- Reported improvements in behaviour, vitality and energy*
- See additional pros in the home-cooked meal section on p. 48

THINGS TO THINK ABOUT

- A quality raw-food diet is typically more expensive than a kibble diet
- It can be easy to neglect certain necessary ingredients for your dog's health when making his food at home, putting him at risk of nutritional deficiency if you're not vigilant or working to an NRC complete and balanced meal plan
- Bacteria cross contamination – meticulous care is required in the handling, preparation and sanitation of raw food
- May not be suitable for sick, immune-compromised dogs and humans who are in contact with the food, especially children and the elderly
- Requires refrigeration or freezing immediately after preparation
- Can't be left out for slow eaters
- Once opened or prepared, the meal should be sealed, refrigerated and consumed generally within 3 days

* Limited robust scientific studies have been done specifically on raw-food diets, but anecdotal evidence from raw feeders supports this, including my own personal experience.

TIPS IF FEEDING A RAW-FOOD DIET

- Check if a raw food product (fresh or frozen), comprises human-grade meat and/or ask about the manufacturing processes used to ensure its safety

- Consult your vet, particularly if your dog is very young or old, or has any health issues, to understand how raw feeding may impact on your dog, their environment and the humans in your household

- Follow safe food handling practices, including washing hands, kitchen tools and workspaces following preparing raw food

- Consider purchasing human-grade meat, if you are making your own. Add the organs and vary the ingredients slightly, particularly meat if your dog has no allergies

- Check the preservation methods. Kangaroo meat is high in sulphur dioxide which may cause thiamine deficiency

- Use recipes formulated to the NRC standards and seek advice from a professional

- Freeze raw meat or poultry until you're ready to use it. Thaw raw meat in your refrigerator or microwave, not in the sink or on the countertop

- If preparing in batches, freeze any portions that will not be consumed within 3 days

- If your pet doesn't finish his food, immediately refrigerate or carefully dispose of the leftovers

- Avoid kissing your dog on or near his mouth, and don't allow him to lick your face

- Transition your dog across to a raw food diet over 7–14 days (*see* pp. 56–57)

- *See* pp. 70–72 for a guide to feeding safe and appropriately-sized bones

DIY RAW FOOD MEALS

While there are a lot of variables to consider relating to the ingredients you should use for your dog, a species appropriate (BARF) diet is broken down into the following:

Raw meat – Raw meat and fats derived from a variety of animals. These provide digestible sources of protein and iron, and make up the largest portion of the diet. Protein is the largest source of amino acids which are used as the basic building blocks of cells in the body. The type of raw meat will depend on your dog, older dogs are better with leaner cuts than what puppies and active dogs may need.

Offal – Organ meat, including liver, kidney, heart, spleen and pancreas, contains proteins and also delivers a plethora of essential vitamins and minerals.

Bone – For concentrated levels of naturally occurring vitamins and minerals, nothing beats soft, non-weight-bearing bones and cartilage for a natural source of calcium and phosphorus for teeth and bone health, zinc for immunity and omega-3 essential fatty acids to reduce inflammation. Again, the balance of these vitamins and minerals is important for your dog, for example a ration of 1:0.7 of calcium to phosphorus is important for orthopaedic development.

Vegetable and fruit matter – These contain a naturally complete range of vitamins and minerals. Mostly green, leafy and coloured vegetables, as well as fruits, ideally crushed and pulped to ensure better absorption. Together these supply antioxidants, phytonutrients, fibre and moisture, as well as essential vitamins and minerals. Cooking the fruit and vegetables, and adding them to the raw matter is recommended to improve their digestibility, and always remove the pips or seeds from the fruit as these may be toxic to dogs.

Other – In the wild this would be fur, stomach lining and organs, like eyes and reproductive organs. In a modern-day version of an evolutionary diet, ingredients like herbs, essential fatty acids, probiotics and prebiotics provide the nutrient profiles of some of these other components without quite so much of the ick factor.

RAW-FOOD DIET RATIOS
Every meal should contain <u>all</u> of the following ingredients:

Muscle meat **70%**	Vegetables **7% or 10%** if no fruit
Organ meat **10%**	Fruit **2%**
Bones **10%**	Supplements **1%**

The meal plan on the following page has been formulated at The Rawsome Effect by their certified raw pet food nutritionist. All meal plans by The Rawsome Effect have been balanced to NRC standards. The amount per day needs to include ALL the ingredients and is based on a 22.5 kg (50 lb) neutered dog considered to have typical activity, so adjust accordingly to suit your dog's weight and exercise levels.

MUST INCLUDE
ALL INGREDIENTS

RAW-FOOD DIET – MEAL PLAN

Macronutrient breakdown

PROTEIN	FAT	CARBOHYDRATES
54%	37%	9%

Calcium to Phosphorus ratio **1.26:1**
Omega 6 to Omega 3 ratio **4.4:1**

INGREDIENTS	COOKED OR RAW	AMOUNT PER DAY
Pork tenderloin	Raw	350 g (12 oz)
Chicken wing	Raw	105 g (4 oz)
Chicken heart	Raw	36 g (1.3 oz)
Chicken thigh	Boneless, skinless, raw	300 g (11 oz)
Beef liver	Raw	12 g (0.4 oz)
Beef tripe	Raw	35 g (1.3 oz)
Oysters	Raw or lightly cooked	12 g (0.4 oz)
Sardine	Raw	75 g (2.7 oz)
Broccoli	Cooked	10 g (0.4 oz)
Asparagus	Cooked	8 g (0.3 oz)
Flaxseed	Ground	1 g (0.04 oz)
Parsley	Fresh	1 g (0.04 oz)
Brewers' yeast		1 g (0.04 oz)
Goat milk yoghurt		4 g (0.2 oz)
Powdered eggshell or coral calcium		4.5 g (0.2 oz)
Vitamin E		100 IU
Organic kelp powder		0.05 g (0.002 oz)

Ingredient notes: Beef liver was added to adjust vitamin A and copper, **chicken thighs** are added for an additional lean meat source, **oysters** are added for zinc and copper, **beef tripe** is added for manganese, **kelp** increases the level of iodine, **vitamin E** should ideally be added as a naturally derived mixed tocopherol supplement.

Home-cooked meals

I come across many dog owners that spend time cooking up a meal for their dogs based around human ingredients and beliefs about nutrition. This often includes beef or chicken mince or muscle meat, frozen vegetables with rice or pasta added and served every day. This diet could be negatively impacting on their dog's health because it lacks all of the essential vitamins and minerals they need in the right balance.

Creating a homemade diet for your dog, whether cooked or raw, requires detailed planning and dedication to ensure you are meeting your dog's dietary needs. To help, refer back to the breakdown of raw food ingredients on the previous page and speak to an animal nutritionist or your vet. Remember to never give your dog cooked bones either!

FOR TIPS ON RAW FOOD DIETS SEE PP. 44–46

THE PROS

- They can be made fresh so that the ingredients retain more of their nutritional value
- If your dog suffers from food allergies, a homemade dog food diet may enable you to control his exposure to the offending ingredient
- Helps limit your dog's exposure to artificial preservatives, flavours, dyes and synthetic vitamins and minerals found in many commercial kibble and wet foods
- You can tailor the ingredients to cater for your dog's preferences
- You can make homemade dog food using many of the ingredients you purchase for yourself and your family already (i.e. fresh meat, vegetables, eggs, fish, etc.)

THINGS TO THINK ABOUT

- Creating a nutritionally balanced homemade dog food requires time and research. It can be difficult to strike the right balance of nutrients to provide a complete and balanced meal, so you need to take the time to understand the formulations and seek out recipes approved by a certified animal nutritionist that meet the NRC standards, as per the raw-food diet
- Cooking the meat can decrease the value of some of the vitamins and minerals found in the raw state, so supplements may be required to reach the required levels
- As it is made fresh, it has a shorter shelf life than commercially prepared dog food
- It may be more expensive than commercial dry dog food

Dehydrated diets

Dehydrated pet food products offer all the benefits of raw, including minimal processing and high bioavailability of nutrients, but use preservation methods that eliminate the pathogens commonly found in raw meats.

Unlike dry kibble and canned food, where the food is cooked at high temperatures to kill the bacteria (and a lot of the nutrients along with it), dehydrated food – including freeze-dry or air-drying methods – is made by eliminating the moisture, which encourages microbial growth, from the raw food ingredients. There is also no need for high levels of carbohydrates to aid the kibble extrusion process.

While they offer some similar benefits and are shelf-stable, nutritious foods with great palatability, there are some differences to note in their preservation processes.

Dehydrated – Dehydration of raw food involves a slow, gentle process of using warm air to remove water or moisture from raw ingredients to preserve them. This process is free of artificial preservatives and still has nutrients and enzymes intact. Dehydrated dog food offers the benefits of a raw diet with none of the preparation (if making your own) or defrosting hassle, making it ideal for travelling, as it is lighter and more nutrient dense than frozen raw, and does not require refrigeration.

Air-dried – Similar to dehydration, air-dried raw-food products provide an extremely nutrient-dense food with scoop and serve convenience. Air-drying involves raw ingredients being placed into drying chambers, where air is continually circulated, this slowly and gently evaporates moisture until it is reduced to a maximum level of 14%. This process eliminates harmful pathogens while preserving vital nutrients, offering nutrition similar to a raw diet.

Freeze-dried – Freeze-drying, like dehydration, is a water removal process which preserves the raw food. While dehydration and air-drying use warm air to remove moisture, freeze-drying works by placing the frozen raw ingredients into a strong vacuum, where the temperature is raised slightly. This causes the frozen water to turn straight into vapour, skipping the liquid phase, and separate from the remaining solid matter. Because 97% of the moisture is removed, freeze-dried foods usually require rehydration before serving. This is extremely important to note. Freeze-drying also preserves more of the nutritional content of the food than dehydrating, as proteins, vitamins and minerals stay intact due to freezing before drying.

THE PROS

- High quality, minimally processed fresh ingredients
- Provide a healthy and safe alternative to a raw-food diet, with preservation methods eliminating the bacteria, whilst retaining much of the value of the enzymes, nutrients, proteins and amino acids
- Good for dogs with poor appetites because they are more palatable
- Convenient and easy to store with stable shelf life without the preservatives
- Do not require refrigeration or freezing
- Great for travelling if taking a frozen raw food product or making your own is not practical
- High in meat protein and bio-nutrients so generally less is required to be fed to your dog each day compared to kibble

THINGS TO THINK ABOUT

- Freeze-dried food MUST be rehydrated with the correct amount of water, and fresh water readily available to your dog or they could face health risks
- Dehydrated, air-dried and freeze-dried dog food is often more expensive than the other food types, particularly so for freeze-dried
- Like any store bought dog food, packaged dehydrated food requires you to trust the manufacturer has used quality ingredients and safe food manufacturing processes, so read the labels
- Ensure you stick to the feeding guides and measurements based on your dog's individual age, size and exercise levels to ensure you do not overfeed
- Dehydrated raw foods may still contain pathogens – so may not be suitable for immunocompromised dogs
- Some freeze-dried dog food is meant for supplemental or intermittent feeding only; always check the label for the complete and balanced diet statement – and read the ingredients list

TIPS FOR USING DEHYDRATED FOOD

- Use freeze- or air-dried raw food products to keep your dog's raw feeding diet consistent when travelling

- Great to use as toppers or mix in with kibble to provide additional nutrition if preparing a raw meat mix is not for you

- Remember to measure the amounts and calorie count of each, and reduce the kibble accordingly to avoid overfeeding if using both

- It is important to provide sufficient water and rehydrate a freeze-dried product, even if only being used as a topper. Kibble has low moisture levels as well, so if you are adding freeze-dried on top of kibble, this is vital

Grain-free/limited ingredient diets

Pet owners who believe their pets suffer from dietary allergies often assume that it must be grains that are the culprit. Yet numerous studies have shown that few dogs have true food allergies alone, and when they do, most intolerances lie with proteins, such as beef, chicken, dairy products and other proteins (*see* p. 19).

If you think your pet has a food allergy, you really do need to talk to your vet and/or a pet nutrition expert so they can help you find the right diet type and ingredients to keep your dog's symptoms at bay, while still providing the balanced nutrition that is essential to good health.

Grain free dry food doesn't mean it doesn't have any carbohydrates. Often starchy vegetables that are lower in fibre and other nutrients are used in high levels to replace the grains, particularly in kibble where the production process relies on some sort of starch to hold the meat and fat together.

There's no evidence gluten is harmful to dogs, with the main exception being some irish setters, which are susceptible to coeliac disease. As with humans, this is where the problem with gluten really lies.

REMEMBER

If you suspect a genuine intolerance, see your vet about undertaking a proper food intolerance test and elimination diet for your pet in relation to gluten.

WOOF!

Vegan and vegetarian diets

In my personal opinion, there are a number of important aspects to consider if you are thinking about feeding your dog a plant-based diet. Firstly, the need to use synthetic vitamins, minerals and other ingredients to supplement the loss of those found naturally in meat-based diets. Secondly, the palatability and digestibility of a vegan diet and, thirdly, the lack of independent research or feeding trials that can demonstrate the long-term health benefits or risks of a plant-based only diet for dogs and cats.

Although this is a book about dogs, I will make mention of cats here as I feel it is important to make a key distinction between the two. Unlike dogs who are considered omnivorous carnivores, cats as a species are obligate carnivores. This means in simple terms, that cats <u>must</u> have meat in their diet.

We also know that regardless of the diet type, dogs and cats need to receive adequate levels of certain nutrients such as proteins, amino acids, vitamins, minerals and certain fats to survive, rather than specific ingredients. So, in theory, a vegetarian or vegan diet that is comprised entirely of plant proteins, minerals and synthetically-based vitamins and other ingredients can provide a dog with their basic nutritional requirements if it is formulated as a complete and balanced diet as per the NRC standards.

However, if a vegetarian or vegan diet for your dog or cat is something you are considering, it is important to weigh up the long-term wellbeing of your own animal against your concern over the welfare of the animals used in pet food production. Talking to your vet about the suitability of a plant-based only diet for your pet based on their individual age, life stage, health and other important factors is a must.

SPECIAL ATTENTION AND REGULAR MONITORING OF URINARY PH IS ESSENTIAL WHEN FEEDING YOUR DOG A VEGETARIAN OR VEGAN DIET

If you are choosing to feed your dog a commercial vegetarian or vegan diet, ask pet food companies what steps they take to ensure nutritional soundness and consistency of batches, and what evidence – particularly independent evidence – they can provide confirming nutritional soundness. Again, this is the same for any commercial pet food, whether meat or plant-based.

Regardless of your own moral concerns or dilemmas, if your dog or cat's health and wellbeing is being compromised on a vegetarian or vegan diet, you may need to consider, at the very least, alternating a complete and nutritionally balanced plant-based meal with a meat-based diet.

At the end of the day, you're responsible for ensuring the health and vitality of your pet, and they rely solely on you to make the right dietary choices to suit their individual needs.

HOW TO CHANGE YOUR DOG'S DIET

Start by introducing small amounts of the new food with the current food, then slowly increasing the new and decreasing the old over a period of approximately 7–14 days, depending on how vast a change you are making, to help avoid stomach upsets.

For example, if you are changing your dog from an inferior kibble to a higher quality kibble, you could do this slowly over 7 days. If your change was more significant, say from a kibble only to a total raw-food diet, you would need to slowly introduce the new diet over a much longer period of time, a minimum of 7 but ideally up to 14 days, as their gut will be undergoing a major shift from a higher gastric alkaline state to more acidic, which is needed to easily digest raw meat and bone.

So, before throwing your kibble-fed dog a raw meaty bone out of the blue, it is important that you gradually introduce small pieces of fresh, quality raw meat or organs into their diet first to prepare their gut for bones and larger quantities of meat.

It will also give them time to get used to any new tastes or textures, and it may also help fussy eaters, or those dogs that aren't into food that much in general. Particularly, transitioning your dog off a low quality, high salt, carb or fat diet to a healthier balanced diet may take longer due to taste.

Watch out for vomit or diarrhoea. Yep, this means monitoring their stools too to make sure everything is coming out the other end okay; no runny

mess, no struggling to go to the toilet, nothing weird or concerning going on.

The common guide for transitioning your dog over to a new diet is:

Day 1–3:	20% new 80% old
Day 4–6:	40% new 60% old
Day 7–9:	60% new 40% old
Day 10–12:	80% new 20% old
Day 12+:	100% new diet

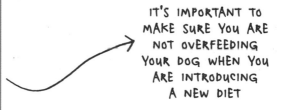

IT'S IMPORTANT TO MAKE SURE YOU ARE NOT OVERFEEDING YOUR DOG WHEN YOU ARE INTRODUCING A NEW DIET

Puppies may take longer to change to a new diet.

Your dog may go through a detoxing period as you wean them off their low quality, nutritionally-poor diet. Symptoms such as watery or runny eyes, dry, flaky skin, excessive shedding of hair, a mucus coating on their stool, or skin conditions are normal and may get worse before they get better. You might even find their stools come out bigger and more pungent, before they become smaller and less stinky if transitioning from a kibble only to raw only for example, so don't be alarmed and give up.

THE RIGHT FOOD FOR YOUR DOG'S AGE

You'd be surprised how many adult dogs I see still being fed a puppy kibble, or a senior dog missing out on a mature formulated diet, both of which could be negatively impacting on their health and comfort. This is why it is so important to take note of the label on the dog food you are buying to make sure it is right for your dog's life stage.

Puppyhood into adolescence

- From birth to at least 12 months puppies need a diet that supports excess energy, as well as growing bones, teeth, muscles and a developing brain

- Puppies are very sensitive to poor quality ingredients, dietary deficiencies and toxins

- Choose a diet specifically formulated for puppies which should have the correct levels of nutrients, especially calcium and phosphorous

- Large breed puppies have different needs to small breeds and large breed puppies have a longer growth period, maturing at 16–18 months

- Most vets recommend making the switch to adult food when your dog reaches about 80% of their full adult size and is moving from adolescence to adulthood. This happens at different times and different ages for different breeds of dogs

Find out from the breeder or foster carer what diet the puppy was on before you take it home. If you want to change your puppy over to a new diet, then it is really important that you do this very slowly (*see* pp. 56–57).

HOW OFTEN TO FEED A PUPPY

🐾 Three equally measured meals

🐾 At the same time every day, ideally 7am, 12pm and 5pm

🐾 Last meal at 5pm to allow digestion and toilet time before bed

🐾 Stick to this basic puppy feeding schedule until the puppy reaches 14–18 weeks old, at which point the meal schedule should change to two meals a day (unless your veterinarian suggests otherwise)

🐾 Even if your puppy is begging for more make sure not to overfeed them. You don't want to set them up to fail by teaching them bad habits during this critical period, such as begging for food

🐾 If your puppy appears to be reluctant about eating food, you might try feeding them inside their crate or in a safe spot so that they can eat without feeling threatened or distracted

PUPPIES TAKE LONGER TO TRANSITION FROM KIBBLE ONLY TO RAW FOOD

Adult dogs

As adult dogs no longer need to fuel rapid growth, they have lower energy needs than puppies. However, some dog breeds are *generally* more active than others, which is reflected by some brands targeting particular breeds or lifestyles. There are both advocates for and against this, but it does stand true that there are some breed considerations to be made when selecting a diet for your adult dog.

Some of the adult large-breed foods, for example, may provide additional sources of glucosamine and chondroitin, the building blocks for healthy joints and cartilage, given a large-breed dog will be carrying an extra load.

As many as one in five dogs will have some form of joint issue or mobility problem, so ensuring they get the nutrients they need to help protect their bones and joints at all life stages is extremely important. Omega-3 fatty acids are good for a dog's skin, coat, brain, nerves and general well-being, no matter the age. Quality proteins help maintain strong, healthy muscles as well.

An adult dog may also have developed a preference for certain flavours, aromas, textures, shapes or kibble size, which is influenced by how they like to chew and swallow their food and/or their sense of smell, which in turn may be affected by their age, health, degree of exposure and their breed.

Brachycephalic dogs (i.e. short or squishy-faced dogs), for example, may have some airway compromise that could affect their sense of smell, which often sees them dubbed as fussy eaters compared to some of the longer nosed breeds that rank high in their smelling abilities (think labradors!).

> Regardless of their breed, preferences or diet type, it is critical dogs receive the complete and balanced diet, and in the right amounts, at all life stages to ensure they remain in good health and condition.

Mature / senior dogs

Our canine buddies generally reach the mature life stage at around 5 years of age for larger dogs and 6–7 years of age for small and medium dogs. Mature or senior dogs tend to slow down as they get older (much like we do!) so mature dog diets are often lower in fat and contain easily digestible proteins to ease the burden on their ageing bodies.

Many diets for older dogs include omega-3 fatty acids from sources including fish oil, green lipped muscles, anti-inflammatory superfoods and supplements including glucosamine and chondroitin to support aging bones and joints. As your dog ages, their risk of kidney disease increases, so low-salt diets are often recommended for mature dogs. Your vet may also recommend supplements to help support cognitive and kidney function.

Poor quality supplements such as some fish oil tablets may also contain high levels of mercury and other toxins, so try sourcing omega-3s and other natural vitamins and minerals from Mother Nature instead, using whole sardines or salmon for example to nourish their bodies, heart and brain.

More studies are also showing the benefits of phytonutrients, which are natural chemicals that are found in fruit and vegetables. They play a role in cellular health, removing toxins from our bodies and even anti-cancer properties, so, if you haven't already, consider slowly introducing some steamed leafy greens and bright orange-yellow vegetables to your ageing dog's diet.

Of course, one of the best things you can do for your ageing dog is to keep them at a healthy weight to help reduce inflammation and the risk of arthritis or putting pressure on their bones and joints. Continuing to exercise them is important for both their mental and physical needs, and as hard as it can be, you may need to reduce their treats as well as they slow down. *See* p. 221 for more information about caring for an elderly dog.

TOXIC FOODS

Alcohol – Ethanol in alcohol is toxic and as pets are much smaller than us, they can be highly affected by just the smallest amounts and may even die. If you suspect your dog has taken a sneaky sip of an alcoholic beverage or you have given them one ☹, keep an eye out for signs such as behavioural changes, excitement, depression, increased urination, staggering and slowed respiratory rate, as this could lead to cardiac arrest and death, and take them straight to the vet at the earliest sign.

Apples, apricots, cherries, peaches and plums – Eating large amounts of stems, seeds and leaves of these fruits can be toxic. They contain a compound similar to cyanide and signs of toxicity include apprehension, dilated pupils, difficulty breathing, hyperventilation and shock. The flesh of the apple is fine and many dogs do love them, just make sure you remove all of the seeds.

Avocados – The toxic component in the avocado is persin. It is not known in what quantities the skin or flesh of the avocado might be toxic for dogs, but the large seed found in the middle of avocados can get stuck in the dog's digestive tract, so it is best to err on the side of caution and keep avocados away from dogs. If you suspect your dog has eaten one, particularly if the seed was included, then seek medical advice.

Baking powder and baking soda – Ingestion of large amounts of baking soda or baking powder can lead to electrolyte abnormalities (low potassium, low calcium and/or high sodium), congestive heart failure or muscle spasms.

Chocolate – In addition to having a high-fat content, chocolate contains caffeine and theobromine. These two compounds are nervous system stimulants and can be fatal to your dog in high amounts. Dogs are not able to metabolise theobromine very quickly which can lead to diarrhea, vomiting, increased urination, muscle twitching, excessive panting, hyperactive behaviour, whining, dehydration, digestive problems, seizures and rapid heart rate. The darker the chocolate, the more dangerous it is – and the smaller the dog, the higher the risk. If you suspect your dog has eaten chocolate call your vet to discuss the type and amount they've consumed, and take them to the clinic at the first sign of any symptoms.

Caffeine, coffee, tea – Caffeine contains the same ingredient contained in chocolate – theobromine. Therefore, you should not allow your dog to drink anything containing caffeine – even some decaffeinated coffee and tea will contain some amounts of theobromine. The symptoms are very similar to those of chocolate toxicity so the same caution and response applies.

Corn on the cob – While corn kernels are not toxic to dogs, corn on the cob is something that results in many dogs being rushed to the vets after digesting the cob, resulting in a blockage in the intestines.

Fatty foods – Rich and fatty foods are favourites of dogs. They often get them as treats, leftovers or from getting into the trash. These fatty foods can cause pancreatitis which is a very painful and serious condition for dogs (see p. 13) that often needs intensive fluid and antibiotic therapy. Signs of pancreatitis generally include an acute onset of vomiting, sometimes diarrhoea, and abdominal pain (they will have a hunched posture or pain when touching their stomach) after digesting fatty foods, so ignore those pleading eyes and keep your dog safe.

Dairy products – Small amounts of plain yogurt or cheese are tolerated by most dogs, but as they lack the enzyme required to digest lactose, dairy can cause digestive issues in some dogs. Dairy products are also high in fat, so if fed too much there is a risk of pancreatitis.

Grapes and raisins – When dogs consume grapes or raisins, it can lead to sudden acute kidney failure and also cause anuria which is a lack of urine production. Watch for vomiting and diarrhoea within the first one

to three hours after ingestion as those are usually the first symptoms of grape or raisin toxicity. If your dog has eaten a large amount for their size, then do take them straight to the vet. Kidney failure develops within approximately 48 hours.

Macadamia nuts – It's a good idea to keep all nuts out of reach of dogs, but macadamias are particularly toxic to dogs. Symptoms may not show up for up to 12 hours following ingestion and are similar to those of alcohol intoxication.

Nutmeg – High levels of nutmeg can be toxic or even fatal in dogs, though it is not certain why. Signs of toxicity include tremors, seizures, nervous system abnormalities or death.

Onions or garlic – Dogs and cats lack the enzyme necessary to properly digest onions and can result in gas, vomiting, diarrhoea or severe gastrointestinal distress. If large amounts of onion or garlic are ingested, including raw, dehydrated, cooked or powders in foods, or if onions are a daily part of your dog's diet, the red blood cells may become fragile and break apart. Signs can begin immediately after eating the onion or a few days later. Severe anaemia and even death can occur if a dog ingests lots of onions or garlic and receives no treatment.

Historically, garlic has been used as a natural remedy to ward off fleas and ticks, treat some skin allergies, prevent infection, and even boost the immune system. However, garlic belongs to the onion family so caution is required. Garlic in very small, controlled amounts can be included in some dog foods. To be safe, avoid giving it to your dog in any homemade meals without first talking to a vet or pet nutritionist about safe levels.

Stones/large seeds in fruits – Although apples, apricots, peaches, mangoes and papaya can provide an array of vitamins and minerals, you need to ensure any seeds, stems and leaves are not given to your dog. Not only can they cause an obstruction in the digestive tract, but ingestion of large amounts of stems, seeds and leaves of these fruits can be toxic. They contain a cyanide-type compound and signs of toxicity include apprehension, dilated pupils, difficulty breathing, hyperventilation and shock. Skip plums and cherries altogether to be safe.

Xylitol (sugar sweetener) – Dogs that eat significant amounts of xylitol can develop a sudden drop in blood sugar, which can cause weakness, lethargy, loss of coordination, collapse and seizures. Symptoms can begin in as little as 30 minutes so see your vet at the earliest sign. Other artificial sweeteners to avoid include aspartame, saccharin and sucralose (and others) as they also have the potential to be very dangerous to your dog.

Yeast dough – When ingested, yeast dough will rise in the stomach just as it would for bread. As the dough rises and ferments, alcohol is produced so it can cause alcohol toxicity, it can also rise to many times its original size, expanding your pet's stomach. Symptoms of vomiting, retching, abdominal discomfort, lethargy or bloat are possible.

WATCH OUT FOR SWEETENERS IN PEANUT BUTTER

BONES

The biggest mistake I see people make with bones is giving their dog cooked bones or inappropriately sized bones. I get really mad at how often I see construction sites littered with lunchtime leftovers of cooked chicken bones. Put your food leftovers in a bin please people, not on the ground. That's called littering and can put animals in danger!

For thousands of years, raw bones have played an important role in a dog's diet. They promote healthy gums and help to keep dogs' teeth clean by scraping off tartar. (They are not the primary way to keep your dog's teeth clean however, *see* p. 198.) They also provide calcium, magnesium phosphorous and other nutrients.

Providing your dog with a recreational bone to chew works out their jaw muscles and also helps your dog with some great mental and physical stimulation.

There are a number of important considerations to keep in mind though when it comes to bones to help ensure your dog gets the most out of them, is kept safe and healthy, and is not put at risk of getting sick or sustaining an injury from them.

NEVER GIVE YOUR DOG COOKED BONES!

Bones must always be given raw, never cooked! Cooked bones can become brittle and splinter, causing potentially fatal internal damage or an intestinal obstruction. You may have done it once before and 'they were fine' but all it takes is for it to go wrong once and you could live to regret it! It's not worth the risk, believe me.

CHOOSING THE RIGHT SIZE

You need to take your dog's size, age, health and temperament into account and choose a bone that matches your dog's size and chewing habits.

BONE TYPE	HOW / WHEN TO USE OR AVOID	TIPS
Raw recreational bones for mental and physical stimulation	Designed to be gnawed on, not chewed up and swallowed entirely as this can throw out the calcium to phosphorous levels in your dog's diet. When a dog chews on a raw meaty recreational bone with cartilage, tendons and soft tissue still attached it can help remove tartar.	Choose a bone large enough so that your dog cannot fit the whole bone in its mouth or swallow the bone whole. Should be meaty so they can strip off the meat before gnawing on it for a while. In general, if your dog eats more of a recreational bone than you intended, just feed him more meat and less bone for the next couple of meals (if you feed a raw diet). This will help to balance out his minerals, including calcium and phosphorus.
Long round versus flat bones	Long round bones are quite hard on the surface so flat bones can be a better choice for medium to large-sized dogs because they're much softer and harder to clamp down on. Large breeds such as german shepherd dogs, bloodhounds and mastiffs should be given large bones.	Bones should be larger than the length of the dog's muzzle so it will be impossible to swallow whole. A raw beef shank bone is a good example of the type of bone to give to a large dog. Long bones have soft ends that are more cartilage than bone, so large, aggressive chewers can tear off a lot of that cartilage which can accumulate in the bowels if he overdoes it, causing blockages or constipation so supervise him and then monitor your dog's bowel movements when feeding bones.

BONE TYPE	HOW / WHEN TO USE OR AVOID	TIPS
Large marrow or leg bones	Avoid large marrow bones with thick outer rims, T-bones, chop bones or those that have been cut lengthwise, such as a leg bone, as they are more likely to splinter or crack teeth.	Avoid.
Raw poultry bones	Poultry bones are for meals, rather than recreational bones. Suited to smaller dogs that can't swallow them whole, so avoid giving to large dogs.	Poultry bones can be crushed or ground to include in a raw-food diet mix for all dog sizes.
Raw bones from smaller animals (i.e. raw lamb neck bones, ribs or flaps)	More suited to smaller to medium sized dogs for an afternoon of chewing.	As with all recreational bones, supervise and monitor your dog's bowel movements.

GENERAL TIPS

- Dogs that chew their bones especially fast or aggressively are at greater risk of doing some damage to their teeth or insides. It's important to check on your dog to make sure he's gnawing on the meat and not chomping down too much bone

- Signs of an intestinal blockage can include bloating, a hunched over posture and frequent unsuccessful attempts to defecate or vomit. If you notice your dog looking uncomfortable, having trouble going to the toilet, or any other abnormal symptoms after eating a bone, then do consult your vet

- Don't leave a bone to dry out and become brittle, or for your dog to bury and potentially dig it up at a later date

- Generally, one or two fresh meaty raw bones may be offered per week, with a few days in between each serving, as too many raw bones may lead to constipation

- Dogs whose teeth are already in poor or weak condition may be at risk of cracking teeth on bones that are too hard, or they might not like chewing them at all due to pain

- Should your dog not be able to or enjoy chewing bones, but you are feeding them a raw-food diet, you'll need to add crushed bones as per the ingredient ratios (*see* p. 45) to provide calcium, phosphorus and trace minerals. Softer, pliable bones like chicken wings and necks that don't contain marrow can be good for this

THINGS TO THINK ABOUT

- You will need to continue with some raw meat in their diet to ensure their pH levels remain in a more acidic state. Dogs who are new to bones, or dogs eating more bones than usual, can suffer from loose stool so keep an eye out for this

- Dogs generally really like bones and can sometimes become protective over them, so take care and discourage young children and others from approaching dogs whilst they are eating bones, or indeed any other food

- Seek out human-grade, raw bones and store them in the freezer, thaw one at a time before feeding to your dog to keep them fresh

THE IMPORTANCE OF WATER

Just like us humans, our dogs are made up of nearly 80% water, so they need access to clean, fresh drinking water to ensure their body can function optimally and to avoid dehydration.

Water aids in the digestion of food, helps the body to absorb nutrients, cools the body down and helps to maintain a normal body temperature. It's needed to cushion and lubricate joints, the spinal cord and other internal tissues, and helps remove toxins from the body.

Without an adequate water supply your dog will become ill and dehydrated, their organs will eventually shut down and they will die if the deficiency lasts longer than a few days. This could occur even quicker in the heat, if your dog is stressed, panting or salivating, or suffering from illnesses like kidney disease, diabetes and cancer, or is pregnant or nursing.

To make sure that your dog always has enough water to keep him healthy, you must provide clean water daily that is easily accessible.

Dogs on a kibble diet will require more water than dogs on wet-canned and raw-food diets because they will receive quite a bit more moisture from their food.

Larger, barrel-chested breeds can be more at risk of bloat, so check they don't gulp down too much water too quickly after exercise. Bloat can be a painful and fatal medical condition, so at the first sign of any discomfort after drinking large amounts of water, it is best to seek medical advice. There may be a heightened risk if they have eaten kibble, are immediately exercised and have gulped down a lot of water, as kibble can swell up to several times its size when it comes into contact with moisture, so may exacerbate the issue.

Ideally supply your dog with filtered water to reduce their exposure to heavily chlorinated water, not to mention the many other toxins now present in our water these days. Our pets are much smaller than we are so can be even more susceptible to these toxins including pharmaceuticals and other drugs, and heavy metals.

Change the water and clean the bowl frequently. Running water like a circulating fountain can keep the water fresh and can also help if your dog is one that likes to splash their water out of their bowl.

If you are concerned that your dog is not getting enough water to maintain health, talk to your veterinarian for advice. Maintaining proper hydration is too important to your dog's health to ignore.

> In general, a 12 kg (26 lb) dog on average needs to drink at least 750 ml to 1.25 litres (3–5 cups) per day, but your dog may need more depending on activity levels, size, age, weather and other influencing circumstances.

TREATS

Talk about a kid in a candy store (or rather a dog in a pet store) when I get to the treat aisles with Darcy! His nose starts twitching as he darts from one shelf to another trying to figure out which of the yummy smells are going to get his full attention. There is so much choice now when it comes to the types of treats available for our dogs, it's enough to send the most chilled out dog into an excited frenzy!

We are now seeing a growing number of treats promising good quality, natural ingredients with vitamins, minerals and other supplements added to support a range of health issues, or a functional purpose such as dental sticks, and much more.

Much in the same way I have talked about reading the ingredients list on dog food labels, you should check what is really inside the packet of the treats you are choosing as well.

Any treats you feed your dog need to be accounted for when you work out their total daily calorie intake. It is imperative that you read the label and understand what you are looking for.

Read the label

Check for an ingredients panel and look to see if meat is the first ingredient, and, like your main pet food ingredients list, avoid those with a long list of names, acronyms or numbers you need a science degree to understand (*see* p. 23).

Dog treats and weight gain

INCLUDE TREATS WHEN CALCULATING YOUR DOG'S DAILY TOTAL CALORIE INTAKE

According to *Forbes* magazine, pet parents are feeding their pets 8—10 treats a day. It doesn't state how much at a time, but even if these are just small pieces of a treat, it is no surprise to me that we are seeing such an obesity epidemic amongst our pets.

It's really important if you treat every day, to limit the amount of treats you feed to about 10% of the total diet. This will help keep your dog lean, but also make sure you don't unbalance their total diet.

It's important to use those treats for a purpose as well. Sure, you can give your dog a treat just to show that you care, but why not make the most of the opportunity and use them to practise some daily obedience with them to keep their minds and bodies active, reward them for when they are being particularly well behaved – rather than just giving a freebie – or use a real meat dehydrated chew that they can gnaw on for a boredom buster as well.

Quality meat and control processes are important

Look for treats made from real meat pieces as a first ingredient and ideally in a human-grade factory, that are low in fat. They should use natural antioxidants and preservatives such as rosemary and vitamin E to maintain product freshness, rather than artificial flavours and preservatives, or synthetic vitamins and minerals, with a low-fat content. Treats that are low in fat are also more likely to be lower in calories.

Puppies and treats

When you get a new puppy, you will certainly come to understand where the phrase 'puppy-dog eyes' comes from. As if it isn't easy enough to spoil a new puppy as it is, try resisting those little eyes staring up at you when they sniff out a treat nearby.

It can be very easy then to lose track of how many treats our puppy may be receiving during training and in general, but it is vital with puppies to make sure you don't overload them. We need to make sure they are getting the right levels of nutrition they need for healthy bones and joints – treats are a supplementary food only, so they can throw out the balance of their diet.

Upset tummies are also more common in puppies. They only have baby teeth, so some of the treats designed for adult dogs may be too hard for them to chew. Just to be safe it's a good idea to have a look at your treat pack and make sure that they can be used for puppies.

Treat safety issues

You should be aware that some types of pet treats have caused health problems (other than obesity) in recent years, for both dogs and the humans handling them. In late 2019 a member alert was issued by the Australian Veterinary Association and the Pet Food Industry Association Australia in relation to kidney failure with variable levels of severity being linked to dehydrated dog food and treats, particularly those made in Asia. Some of the dogs recovered once they stopped having the treats and they received treatment from a vet. However, some of the cases were severe enough to cause fatal renal failure and the dogs died. At this time, and despite extensive investigation, the actual toxin that causes the disease is still unknown. That's why it is important to read the label and talk to the manufacturer if you have any concerns. Some of the treats include:

PIGS' EARS

In 2019 a salmonella outbreak across the US was linked to pig ear dog treats and chews which resulted in a nationwide recall. Several strains of salmonella were found on pig ear treats and chews from many different suppliers in the US and other countries. Hundreds of people, including children, became sick after touching the treats or caring for dogs who ate them.

Even if you are choosing premium, 100% natural, or even organic versions, it is imperative that you protect yourself by always washing your hands after handling them (as with any dog treat or food!) and after touching your dog to avoid any chance of salmonella contamination. Keep the treats away from children, the elderly or anyone that is unwell.

If your dog is small, old or has soft jaws (like many smaller retrievers), or is required to be on a low-fat diet, then it is also advisable to avoid pigs' ears.

REMEMBER
If you are purchasing products such as pig's ears for your dog make sure you do your research and consider their source. Recognise that many imported or cheap pig's ears aren't guaranteed 100% animal product – often they may have additives and chemicals that could impact on your dog's health, while others may pose a salmonella risk.

RAWHIDE BONES AND CHEWS

Hard   Shaped   Twisted   Treats

SOME TOXIC CHEMICALS HAVE BEEN FOUND IN RAWHIDE BONES AND CHEWS

Rawhide bones and chews are also a popular treat used to keep dogs occupied, but you need to be aware of some additives which may be toxic.

Rawhide is the inner soft hide or skin of an animal. It is most commonly made from cows but technically it can be made from any cleft-hoofed livestock. Many of the cheap, heavily processed versions are treated with a chemical to help preserve the product, before being bleached or having dyes, glues and flavours used to provide them with their shape, colour and taste. Some toxic chemicals that have been found in some rawhide bones and chews include lead, arsenic, mercury, formaldehyde and others.

Again, there can be a vast difference in quality, ingredients used and levels of toxic chemicals, glues and other materials used to bind them together depending on the shape, so contact the manufacturer to find out exactly what you can expect to find in the rawhide chew you are choosing.

If you can't find any contact details for the source of the product, err on the side of caution and search out an alternative, or opt for a real raw meaty bone instead.

TREATS – FINAL TIPS

🐾 Always supervise your dog when they are eating a treat

🐾 Watch for choking or intestinal blockages

🐾 Include treats in total calorie count

🐾 Consider making homemade treats (*see* pp. 88–92 for recipes)

HELP! MY DOG ISN'T EATING

There can be a number of reasons for a dog not eating their food and often it has a lot to do with what we owners are doing. If your dog doesn't seem to like a new food you are serving, or they are a fussy eater in general, you may find you are overfeeding them, giving them too many treats or encouraging them to become fussy without realising it.

Fussy eaters

It's believed that fussy eaters don't always have an issue with the taste or smell of their food but rather they are smart dogs holding out for something more delicious. Sound familiar? I've been caught out doing this myself, so I know how easily it is done. We resort to dropping in some different bits of food into their meal like mince, cheese, chicken or bits of treats to encourage them to eat, all of which are high-value rewards for dogs, so you're actually reinforcing the behaviour and they start to learn that by holding out on their normal food, some better options will soon follow.

If your dog is already receiving a high quality, complete and balanced meal that they generally eat when hungry, then simply take the food away if they don't consume it within half an hour. Do not give your dog any other food, treats or snacks until it's time for his next meal. If you feed meals at a regular time each day, monitor how much you feed them so they are not overfed, this will go a long way to curbing the fussy eating.

Tummy upsets

Consistency is key with dogs in terms of the diet type you are feeding them so the more you mess around with their food, the more likely your dog is to suffer from gastrointestinal upsets. If this happens, they may stop eating, which will make you want to try another food, leading to more tummy upsets and so it goes on.

Also, some pet dogs just love stealing food from the table, rubbish or a smelly scrap found at the park, so sometimes they simply eat things they shouldn't. If you're sure you are not encouraging your dog's fussiness, it is possible he could have a temporary gastrointestinal upset, so check around for some diarrhoea or if he has vomited somewhere. Provide plenty of water and keep an eye out for any of the other symptoms listed in the toxic food section. If the vomiting or diarrhoea lasts more than 24 hours or you notice blood in their stool, then take your dog to the vet.

Change in routine

A change in routine such as the time you feed or walk them, moving house, going away on holiday, bringing a new baby home ... anything that might throw out their routine or what they are familiar with can upset many dogs and cause them to stop eating, until they feel secure again. It's best to keep any changes to their routine gradual, make sure that your dog has a safe, quiet place to eat and is positively reinforced with praise when they start to look out for or sniff their food.

FUSSY EATERS ARE OFTEN SMART DOGS HOLDING OUT FOR SOMETHING DELICIOUS

Stress and anxiety

Similar to a change in routine, some dogs may not eat when left alone due to separation anxiety. You could feed them when you get home and they are feeling safe and comfortable. (*See* pp. 202–203 for more about anxiety.) If you have a multiple pet household they may be reacting to the other dog or pet.

If you have multiple dogs, it's often a good idea to feed them separately so each dog can eat in peace. Dogs will often start eating again when they are left alone with their food. I see this often with other people's dogs coming in and out of Pooches HQ and make sure I provide Darcy with his own space to eat as he can be a slow eater, and likes to feel safe and secure when he eats his meal. Also look for things like cold drafts, noises that might be nearby, their tag clinking on the bowl, etc. Basically ... think like a dog and consider how you might feel uncomfortable if something was bothering you while you are trying to focus on eating, and you were nervous or didn't want to let your guard down.

Older dogs/loss of senses

If you have a senior dog you may find they stop eating because of age-related problems including a decrease in their sense of smell or dental problems. Don't assume he is just losing his appetite because he is old. Try warming the food or topping it with some meat and veggies (transitioning this in slowly over 14 days, bit-by-bit if you haven't already been adding it in their diet) so that the smell and taste is stronger and more appealing as their senses begin to fade.

Sore or rotten teeth

Gum disease and rotten or sore teeth could also be a reason for a lack of appetite so definitely visit your vet if your older dog is starting to go off his meals. In fact, always check your dog's breath and teeth for anything that might be going on there if they suddenly stop eating and none of the other reasons apply.

These are just some of the key reasons, outside of illness, for why your dog may not be eating, so if you are still having issues and your dog won't eat after 24 hours, then do take him to your vet for a check-up, as there may be something more serious going on that requires immediate medical attention.

DOG FEEDING CHECKLIST

HOW OFTEN/WHEN TO FEED

- Feed your dog once a day or twice a day with smaller meals, just keep it consistent
- Feed puppies three times a day – morning, noon and early evening
- Deep-chested breeds such as the doberman can benefit from two smaller meals

HOW TO AVOID BLOAT

- Bloat is a serious, life-threatening condition that always requires immediate veterinary attention
- Do not feed your dog an hour before or after energetic exercise as this can cause twisting of the gut and blocking of the stomach which is known as bloat
- Many dogs, but particularly deep-chested breeds, are susceptible to bloat, but it can affect all breeds
- Likewise, don't let them guzzle down large amounts of water too quickly during or after exercise

READ THE LABELS

- Read the labels to understand the nutrient value of the food you choose (*see* p. 23)

🐾 Follow the feeding guide on the back of the packaging, but remember the guide is only there to give you an idea. Every dog is an individual, so the most important consideration is to feed enough with the right nutrition to maintain a lean, healthy condition

STORAGE

🐾 Serve food at room temperature to ensure your dog can taste and smell it properly

🐾 If feeding a raw food diet don't leave it out too long, or in the heat or sun

🐾 Be mindful of cross-contamination when handling raw meat, keep it separate from cooked or processed food

🐾 If feeding a dry, complete food, store it in a dry, clean environment in resealable packaging or an airtight container and use by the best before date

🐾 Canned wet and raw food should be stored in the fridge, in an airtight container and consumed within 3 days

SAFETY

🐾 Your dog should be fed in a quiet place away from interruptions and away from where you eat

🐾 Don't allow children to interrupt your dog when he is eating or he may react aggressively – this is known as resource guarding. If you have a puppy you can help avoid this by regularly taking away their meal and praising them for allowing you to do so, before immediately giving it back with more praise to create a positive association with their food being touched or taken away whilst eating

- 🐾 If you have more than one dog, feed them separately to avoid bullying or resource guarding if they have not been conditioned to eat with other dogs

RESPONSIBLE FEEDING

- 🐾 If you feed biscuits or treats, remember to reduce your dog's main meals accordingly. Keep them to no more than 10% of your dog's calorie intake

- 🐾 Avoid fatty human scraps or toxic food

- 🐾 Raw chunks of vegetables can't be absorbed properly by your dog and can lead to weight gain if given on top of their daily limit. Instead, use a blender to pulp or steam them before adding to your dog's meal

- 🐾 Transition to a new diet over 1–2 weeks (*see* pp. 56–57)

- 🐾 Cat food doesn't provide dogs with the essential nutrients they need and cats should never be fed dog food. Feed species-appropriate food only to your pets

- 🐾 Provide plenty of clean fresh drinking water. Avoid heavily chlorinated water if possible

SLOWING DOWN FAST EATERS

- 🐾 If you have a dog that is a fast eater, use a slow feeding bowl

- 🐾 Even better, throw their kibble around the yard, or place meat/wet food in small batches on bowls around the garden or room so that they have to hunt out their food like they would in the wild

THIS IS A GREAT WAY TO SLOW DOGS DOWN AND PROVIDES ADDITIONAL MENTAL AND PHYSICAL STIMULATION

RECIPES

CHICKEN, SWEET POTATO AND STRAWBERRY TREATS
MAKES 50 TREATS

This recipe has been formulated at The Rawsome Effect by their certified raw pet food nutritionist. Visit www.therawsomeeffect.com for more recipes.

Not only is sweet potato good for us, it's good for your dog too. Sweet potato is a source of important nutrients including iron, calcium, zinc and potassium as well as being high in fibre and low in fat and sodium. The chicken provides much needed protein and strawberries are full of antioxidants and vitamin C.

YOU WILL NEED

2 baking trays
greaseproof baking paper
large bowl
wooden spoon
  (or similar for mixing)
rolling pin
4.5 cm (1½ inch) cookie cutter
wire cooling rack

INGREDIENTS

1 cup **chicken** (diced and cooked)
1 cup **sweet potato**
  (peeled, cooked and mashed)
½ cup **strawberries**
  (washed and finely chopped)
extra sliced strawberries
  for decoration
3 tsp **fresh mint** (chopped)
  or 1 tsp dried mint
1 cup **coconut flour**
extra coconut flour to help with
  rolling out the mixture
1 cup **water**

METHOD

🐾 Preheat oven to 160°C (320°F)

🐾 Line two baking trays with greaseproof baking paper

🐾 In a large bowl mix the cooked and diced **chicken**, mashed **sweet potato**, chopped **strawberries**, **mint** and **coconut flour**

🐾 Once mixed together add the **water** and mix until all the ingredients are combined

🐾 Sprinkle a little extra coconut flour onto a flat surface. Place the mixture on the floured surface and sprinkle with a little more flour as needed to stop it sticking

🐾 Roll out the mixture to 5 mm (¼ inch) thickness

🐾 Use the cookie cutter to cut the mixture into bite sized treats

🐾 Place the treats onto the baking trays

🐾 Lightly place a slice of **strawberry** onto each biscuit

🐾 Place the trays into the pre-heated oven and bake for 25–30 minutes, or until golden brown

🐾 Remove the treats from the oven and after letting them sit for a few minutes, carefully move them to the wire cooling rack

In an airtight container the treats will last 5 days if kept in the refrigerator.

They can also be frozen in an airtight container for 3 months.

CHICKEN LIVER, ZUCCHINI, TURMERIC & BASIL BISCUIT TREATS
MAKES 24 TREATS

This recipe has been formulated at The Rawsome Effect by their certified raw pet food nutritionist. Visit www.therawsomeeffect.com for more recipes.

Chicken liver is highly nutritious for dogs, although it should be served in moderation, and it is perfect for a treat. Zucchini (courgette), is low in calories, turmeric is known for having anti-inflammatory properties and basil has qualities thought to help prevent cancer and arthritis.

YOU WILL NEED

2 baking trays
greaseproof baking paper
large bowl
wooden spoon
  (or similar for mixing)
rolling pin
4.5 cm (1½ inch) cookie cutter
wire cooling rack

INGREDIENTS

1 cup **chicken liver**
  (cooked and chopped)
½ cup **zucchini (courgette)**
  (grated)
extra grated zucchini for
  decoration
¼ cup **cottage cheese**
1 tsp dried **turmeric** powder
6 leaves fresh **basil**
  (or 1 tsp dried basil)
1 cup **lentil flour**
extra lentil flour to help with
  rolling out the mixture
¼ cup water

METHOD

- Preheat oven to 160°C (320°F)
- Line two baking trays with greaseproof baking paper
- In a large bowl mix the cooked and diced **chicken liver**, grated **zucchini**, **cottage cheese**, **turmeric**, **basil** and **lentil flour**
- Once mixed together add the **water** and mix until all the ingredients are combined
- Sprinkle a little extra lentil flour onto a flat surface. Place the mixture on the floured surface and sprinkle with a little more flour to stop it sticking.
- Roll out the mixture to 5 mm (¼ inch) thickness
- Use the cookie cutter to cut the mixture into bite sized treats
- Place the treats onto the baking trays
- Lightly place a little extra grated **zucchini** onto each biscuit
- Place the trays into the pre-heated oven and bake for 20–25 minutes, or until golden brown
- Remove the treats from the oven and after letting them sit for a few minutes, carefully move them to the wire cooling rack

In an airtight container the treats will last 5 days if kept in the refrigerator.

They can also be frozen in an airtight container for 3 months.

HOMEMADE PEANUT BUTTER
MAKES 1 CUP

This recipe has been formulated at The Rawsome Effect by their certified raw pet food nutritionist. Visit www.therawsomeeffect.com for more recipes.

Peanut butter is a great treat for dogs as it contains lots of nutrients in the form of healthy fats, vitamins, minerals and antioxidants. There are a few things to be aware of: only use raw, dry-roasted, unsalted peanuts, these are the only safe peanuts to use. Salted peanuts are too high in sodium for dogs and other nuts such as macadamias, walnuts or brazil nuts can make your dog very unwell and may lead to their death – so unsalted raw peanuts only please!

YOU WILL NEED

Blender or food processor
Airtight container/glass jar with lid

INGREDIENTS

2 cups **dry-roasted or raw, unsalted peanuts**

optional extras:
1 tbs **ground flaxseeds**
1 tbs melted **coconut oil**
1 tbs **honey**

METHOD

- 🐾 Place the **peanuts** (and the **optional extras** if desired) in the blender or food processor
- 🐾 Blend the ingredients until they are the desired consistency, this may take around 4 minutes
- 🐾 Once the peanut butter is smooth remove it with a spatula from the blender and place it into an airtight container

Making peanut butter may cause your blender to overheat so you may need to turn it off for a couple of minutes if the motor gets hot.

If refrigerated in an airtight container the homemade peanut butter will last a month.

BIRTHDAY CAKE RECIPES

STRAWBERRY AND BUCKWHEAT CAKE

This recipe has been formulated at The Rawsome Effect by their certified raw pet food nutritionist. Visit www.therawsomeeffect.com for more birthday recipe ideas.

The ingredients for this cake provide vitamins and nutrients as well as antioxidants and anti-inflammatories which help with overall health. The coconut oil is hydrating for their skin and will help if your dog has dandruff or dry skin.

YOU WILL NEED

13 cm (5 in) cake tin
large bowl
wooden spoon, or similar
  for mixing
wire cooling rack

INGREDIENTS

½ cup **strawberries**
extra strawberry for topping
1 cup **buckwheat flour**
extra buckwheat flour for topping
2 **eggs**
2 tbs **coconut oil** (melted)
extra coconut oil for greasing
  the tin
1 tsp **ground cinnamon**

METHOD

- Preheat oven to 175°C (350°F)
- Grease cake tin using extra coconut oil
- Place **all the ingredients** in a large bowl and mix until combined
- Pour mixture into cake tin
- Bake in preheated oven for 30–35 min or until golden brown
- Remove from the oven and let sit for a few minutes before turning onto the wire cooling rack
- Once the cake has cooled, sprinkle with extra buckwheat flour and top with extra strawberry

The cake will last 2 days if you place it in an air-tight container in the refrigerator or can be frozen for up to 3 months.

NAKED PEANUT BUTTER AND CAROB DOG CAKE WITH GREEK YOGHURT ICING

(Recipe provided by Willows Pantry, Melbourne)

IF YOU WANT TO TAKE YOUR BAKING TO A WHOLE NEW LEVEL, CHECK OUT THIS AWESOME BIRTHDAY CAKE FROM WILLOWS PANTRY IN MELBOURNE, AUSTRALIA, WHO KINDLY PROVIDED THIS RECIPE

YOU WILL NEED

13 cm (6 in) cake tin
non-stick spray
bread knife
piping bag & nozzle
20 cm (8 in) cake board
cake rack
bench/dough scraper
metal cake spatula
optional: cake turntable
mixer or food processor

INGREDIENTS

2 **eggs**
100 g (3½ oz) **apple sauce** (if using commercially produced sauce look for no added sugar, sweeteners, preservatives or other additives)
1 **banana** (mashed)
100 g (3½ oz) **peanut butter** (see recipe or only use a commercial one with NO xylitol or other artificial sweeteners)
100 ml (3½ fl oz) **water**
300 g (10 oz) **buckwheat flour** (or other dog safe flours including rice flour, coconut flour, almond, lentil or barley flour)
30 g (1 oz) carob drops, chopped into small pieces

Icing:
200 g (7 oz) **peanut butter** (ensure peanut butter does not have added xylitol or other sweeteners)
150 g (5 oz) **greek yoghurt**

METHOD

- Preheat oven to 160°C or (320°F)
- Spray cake tin with non-stick spray
- Place **eggs, apple sauce, banana, peanut butter** and **water** in mixer or blender
- Add **buckwheat flour** and **carob** and mix to a smooth batter
- If the batter is too stiff, add a bit of water
- Fill cake tin to two thirds full and bake for about 40 min
- Check the cake during cooking by poking a skewer into it. If it comes out clean without batter streaks, your cake is done (a few crumbs are ok).
- While the cake is happily baking away, mix **peanut butter** and **greek yoghurt** together
- Fill a piping bag with icing and keep it in the fridge
- Take cake out of the tin and let cool down on a rack (or place it in the fridge, if you're in a hurry)

ASSEMBLING & DECORATING

- Slice cake evenly into 2 layers (horizontally)
- Dab a bit of icing onto a cake board to attach the first cake layer
- Spread a thin layer of icing onto the cake and place the other cake layer with the cut side down on top of the icing
- Refrigerate for 30 min
- Spread the remaining icing thickly and evenly over the entire cake with a large metal cake spatula
- Use a bench/dough scraper to smooth out the sides and take excess icing off
- You can use a cake turntable or simply turn the cake itself around on an upside-down cake tin
- Use piping bag to decorate cake

TIPS: *For natural colours mix a bit of turmeric, beetroot powder or blueberries into your icing. As decorations you can use dog cookies, banana chips, blueberries, desiccated coconut or chopped peanuts.*

PLAY

THE IMPORTANCE OF PLAY AND TRAINING

Some of the most common dog behaviour issues that I deal with as a dog trainer are a result of poor early socialisation and/or because the dogs are lacking the levels of physical and mental stimulation they need. They are left alone all day while owners go out to work. They're bored or anxious and are just not getting enough play in their lives.

Scientists agree: a Bristol University study of 4000 dog owners showed that dogs who don't engage in a lot of play suffer from one or more of 22 behavioural problems, including anxiety and aggression. Less play time also leads to an increase in whining, jumping up, and a lack of recall.

Think about what the wolves and wild canines would be doing – out hunting all day for their food, keeping both physically and mentally fit, while our domestic canines languish their days away in suburbia with nothing to do. It's even worse for our working dog breeds that would normally be running around all day herding, chasing, scenting, retrieving, hunting and fulfilling their instinctual needs.

A great way to add some extra stimulation and strenghen your bond with your dog is by adding more play into their day. Everything about dog training and human–canine interactions comes down to the relationship you have with your dog.

BONDING TAKES TIME AND EFFORT

For my little dog Darcy this means two daily walks, plenty of interaction with other furry friends, brain games, obedience training and other environmental enrichment. It's not easy, when you have to go out to work

all day, so, for that reason, I've compiled some tips and activities that can help you get more play into your dog's life. Not to mention your own!

Dogs are good for our health, both mental and physical, so why not get out and play with your dog more? You'll reap the benefits in return!

Why do dogs like playing?

Another Bristol University study showed that dogs play because it helps them learn motor skills like rolling and tugging, while also teaching them how to stop when a bite is no longer playful. It helps to build social relationships with other dogs and strengthens the human–animal bond.

With limited mental or physical stimulation we see destructive behaviour such as digging, chewing, barking, and a rise in anxiety and other phobias. By recognising your role in keeping unwanted behaviours at bay and spending more time each day playing with your dog, you will improve the mental and physical wellbeing of both you and your dog.

How much play your dog needs, comes down to his individual needs, and what other exercise and mental stimulation he is getting throughout their day (or not!). Even if you take your dog for a walk, this doesn't always mean he is getting in the play time he needs.

Dogs will do pretty much anything if there is the promise of a reward and that doesn't always have to be food. Those who train dogs to carry out the most demanding of tasks such as drug or explosive detection, search and rescue, and snake avoidance training often use play as a reward over food. That's how appealing play in the form of a game of tug or ball can be to a dog.

BUILDING A BOND THROUGH PLAY

If your dog isn't interacting or listening to you, a good place to start is working on strengthening your bond through play. A strong bond is one where your dog respects and trusts you because they know if they cooperate with you, good things happen.

> Owners who form a strong bond with their dogs are more inclined to train them, and trained dogs are more likely to be included in family activities and outdoor adventures.

If your dog loves learning (as many do) training is also a wonderful way to bond. Teach him entertaining tricks such as waving, walking backwards, rolling over, speaking and high-fiving. Not only is training fun and interactive, but it also teaches him problem-solving and body awareness while improving his fitness. Training doesn't always have to be a laborious task or require large amounts of your time each day.

Even though I am a certified dog trainer, I have to admit that between other dogs coming in and out, filming of the show and other work commitments, I don't spend a lot of time on formal training with Darcy, but I do make sure I do some short bursts of obedience training each day – even just incidental basics such as 'sit', 'recall', 'stay' and 'on your mat.' Even small amounts of daily training and obedience are very important in creating good leadership, building your bond, reinforces desired behaviour and keep your dog safe. However, we sure do a lot of play, and this has had a big role in how he responds to my commands and the level of attention and obedience I can get from him when I want or need it.

So many people say what a good, well-trained little dog Darcy is which makes me chuckle, as he still has a very strong innate desire to chase after balls and magpies, and rush at some dogs who are on-lead when he is off-lead, which is a reinforced behaviour from before I owned him. However, because I know how much he loves to play with balls and anything squeaky, I can easily use his overriding motivation and desire for play as a way to distract, stop and redirect his attention when I need to.

Our play has also helped me work on his noise phobias, which a lot of dogs have (think fireworks, thunderstorms and loud noises in general), as I know I can tap into his strong desire to play with a tennis ball or a squeaky toy to help create a positive association with a negative situation or trigger, such as when a loud noise he is likely to react to occurs. In this way, I am using play as part of his desensitisation program to help him overcome his noise phobia ... or at least cope better when the trigger (a loud noise) occurs.

So, as I hope you are starting to see, play is more than just spoiling your dog with a bit of extra attention. It actually serves a very important and useful purpose in building a good bond with your dog. In turn, this helps keep them engaged, mentally and physically stimulated, fulfilled and happy, while also helping with your obedience training for the benefit of everyone!

HOW DOGS PLAY WITH EACH OTHER

The crazy antics of tag and chase, wrestling, biting, chasing, rolling and running around until exhausted might sometimes look the same as when two dogs fight, but the frenetic, repetitive, fast pace of play is much more random. It is how dogs know that they are indeed playing and not trying to instigate a fight.

Dogs' minds are very active, and they are able to process information rapidly and accurately, even on the run, which is how play remains playful!

When dogs of different sizes play together, a larger dog may hold back or self-handicap to ensure that its size and strength doesn't result in conflict or injury. Dogs know they have to play fair and by doing this they can keep the game going, which is far more important than winning the battle.

Some dogs role reverse. A naturally dominant dog may happily roll over on their back during play, an action they would not do in a fight. It's really important that both dogs give and take in play, reversing the roles so that the game is fair and they take turns in winning and losing.

Dogs exhibit four basic aspects of fair play:

1. Ask first

2. Be honest

3. Follow the rules

4. Admit when you're wrong

Dogs keep track of what is happening when they play. They can read what other dogs are doing, and they trust that others want to play rather than fight.

GEE, DON'T WE WISH THIS WENT ON MORE IN OUR HUMAN WORLD?

NORMAL PLAY ACTIONS

- Bowing (known as the play bow)

- Face pawing

- Approaching and rapidly withdrawing (tag and chase)

- Dodging left to right

- Mouthing or biting the other dog but not aggressively

- Even running right at a potential playmate

The play bow is when a dog crouches on forelimbs and is sometimes accompanied by barking and tail wagging. This is a clear invitation to the other dog to play and helps to change the meaning of any other actions that are to follow, such as biting or mouthing, that might otherwise be seen as threatening or aggressive behaviour. After there has been a pause for rest, a play bow can then also restart the play.

THE PLAY BOW

Sometimes it can look like two dogs in the full throes of play are fighting or about to fight, but as long as they are being fair, taking turns and mimicking each other, any real conflict is usually avoided. It is a good idea however to keep an eye out when there is a big size or age gap that may result in one of them accidentally hurting the other – if they start to get a bit too aroused as their adrenaline levels rise, or another dog decides to get in on the act.

If things do get a little intense or one is tiring a bit, you might notice one of the dogs instigating a time out signal that provides them both with a short break and lets the other dog know that things are still cool between them.

TIME-OUT SIGNALS

🐾 Stops playing and sniffs or sneezes

🐾 Stops playing and gives themselves a scratch or lick

🐾 Stops playing and gives a shake off

Darcy tends to stop and give himself a shake off if things get a bit rough or have gone a little too far, and usually the other dog will do this too so they both have a moment to cool down and let each other know it's all okay.

If a puppy or adult dog hasn't had enough socialisation or opportunity to play with other dogs, and they don't know how to read the signals properly, they play too rough or have a lack of manners (mounting can be a form of bad manners and inappropriate play), other dogs may react negatively. This is why it is so important to ensure you socialise your dog early as a puppy, or work with a trainer or local obedience club, to teach your dog the rules of engagement with other dogs.

> Socialisation is how dogs learn to interact with other dogs, people and objects.

WANNA PLAY?

SOCIALISATION – IT'S ESSENTIAL FOR PUPPIES

Your puppy will usually remain with his mum and littermates until he is at least 8 weeks old so he can learn to be a dog! When you do get your puppy home it is very important that you begin socialising him straight away. This means teaching him how to respond to his environment as well as getting him out and playing with other dogs. You should introduce him to different types of people – different sizes, ages, races and looks (i.e. with glasses, in hats or hoods) – and different places, so that they get familiar in a positive way with a variety of situations and different types of people. Everything a dog learns in the first 3–16 weeks of its life, known as the Socialisation Period, is permanent and will be retained in the memory of the dog for life. Therefore a dog that has had the right experiences during this time is far more prepared for dealing with the world around it, while a dog with limited or negative associations during this time will be less prepared and may be prone to fear and phobias, aggression and other behavioural issues.

A good puppy class is an excellent way to introduce your puppy to other dogs and should include opportunities for play. Play should be a positive experience, so ensure you and the dog trainer monitor it carefully. If you are not sure if your puppy is enjoying it, do a consent test – separate the puppies and see if they both want to return to play or not.

Socialisation with objects and noises

Darcy used to react to thunderstorms by turning into a trembling mess until I tapped into his intense desire to play with a tennis ball or squeaky toy! So helping your dog to deal with objects and noises is essential. Some of the common items dogs react to include lawnmowers, bikes, skateboards, vacuums, cars, loud noises, thunderstorms and firework sounds. You should also expose your puppy to different floor types, puddles, gravel etc. I've seen many dogs that are afraid of walking on slippery floors, which can be due to a lack of exposure, and it can be a tough phobia for you both to deal with should you move to a new home that has tiles or floorboards!

If they are slowly and positively introduced to these experiences, as a puppy, then you can avoid having an adult dog on your hands that is constantly barking or chasing after skateboards, wheels or the vacuum, or that turns into a trembling mess when they sense a thunderstorm coming, like Darcy.

For any training or behaviour modification it is important that you know what your dog is motivated by (loves) the most, as all dogs are different. Some prefer food or praise, squeaky toys or a ball, or a game of tug.

I cannot stress how important early and proper socialisation is for your puppy, as is finding the right trainer or puppy socialisation class. The best way to find a good trainer or puppy school is to contact a government-approved dog training organisation, ask the owners of particularly well-behaved dogs or puppies at your local dog park, or through your local Facebook community groups.

USE THIS PROCESS FOR ANYTHING YOUR DOG MIGHT REACT TO

HOW TO INTRODUCE YOUR NEW PUPPY TO A VACUUM

1. Start with the vacuum turned off

2. Encourage your puppy to sniff and explore it

3. Reward him for calm interaction (or even disinterest) with a treat, praise or play (depending on what he loves most) to create a positive association and reinforce that desired behaviour

4. Do this a few times until you are sure they are comfortable being around the vacuum without reacting

5. If your puppy barks or backs away, don't react. Increase the distance, but so the vacuum remains in view, and reward them once calm. Work slowly to decrease the distance with no reaction

6. When you are confident your puppy is ready, again start at a distance and move the vacuum around while still turned off. Ideally have someone help you with the next few steps, and continue rewarding no reaction

7. Again, if your puppy reacts, go back a step and start with even more distance the next time

8. Follow the same two steps above to progress to having the vacuum turned on and still, then turning it on and moving it

9. Should your puppy try to bite or actively play with the vacuum at any of the stages, verbally "shoo" them away (do NOT use the vacuum to physically do this) and reward them for calm behaviour *away* from the vacuum ... and keep going back a step if you need to

10. Try this technique with some of the most common items that dogs can be reactive to including lawn mowers, leaf blowers, hair dryers etc.

HOW TO MANAGE A LACK OF SOCIALISATION IN ADULT DOGS

You may have adopted an older dog that was kept locked up or was constantly exposed to negative social situations. Your own dog may have had a bad experience as a puppy and has formed a negative association with something, so it is important that you can identify the signs that indicate your adult dog is in need of some safe and positive socialisation or desensitisation to certain triggers.

SIGNS YOUR DOG IS STRESSED OR SCARED

FOR A GUIDE TO DOG BODY LANGUAGE SEE PP. 117–122

- Folds his ears back
- Tucks his tail under his body
- Tongue flicks rapidly
- Yawns
- Cowers or backs away

- Lowers his body
- His top lip curls slightly, he may even show some teeth
- He emits a low growl
- Barks and lunges as soon as they catch sight of another dog or person

Re-introducing an adult dog to the world around them with proper socialisation can be difficult and requires a lot of patience, positive reinforcement and good leadership. Depending on the size and breed, it can even become dangerous if they become aggressive. To help, here are some tips on how to safely socialise your adult dog that hasn't had the best start in life. I strongly recommend getting the help of a certified and experienced trainer if your dog is extremely reactive to ensure you do not make the situation worse.

Use a properly fitted muzzle

If your dog has a tendency to become aggressive around other dogs, having your dog wear a comfortable and properly fitted muzzle can help prevent an injury. You might not plan on letting your dog off the lead or near other dogs, but unfortunately there are still too many dog owners that don't or can't keep their own dog under effective control. Often they are ignorant that they could be placing their own friendly dog in danger by letting it run up to other dogs that may have aggression issues.

Avoid reinforcing their fear

Whenever your dog becomes frightened and reacts, don't reinforce it. Rather than making a fuss and trying to actively soothe them with sympathetic sounds, hugs, pats etc., ignore your dog's anxious behaviour and instead act calm and relaxed showing him in the process that there's nothing to be afraid of.

Reward him for calm behaviour in the face of adversity as this is what you want to be reinforcing. Remember any behaviour you reward (which includes giving your dog attention or touching him when he is demanding it or acting anxious) will reinforce that behaviour and it will occur with more frequency and intensity. Please note, that I am not recommending to simply ignore it if their reaction is quite severe or they are acting out with aggression, that is likely to require professional help.

WALKING NERVOUS OR AGGRESSIVE DOGS

🐾 **Walk early in the morning and late at night**

Assuming your dog can cope and still enjoys exercise outside of the home, you may finding taking him out early in the morning and later at night when you are less likely to encounter lots of dogs and people, can help to slowly build up their interactions in a positive way.

🐾 **Keep calm, don't pick them up or jerk on the lead**

When you see others approaching in the distance, ensure *you* keep calm and provide good leadership so your dog can be confident you have everything under control. Don't panic and pick him up (which will reinforce their fear) or jerk on the lead or yell at him if he starts to react (which increases the negative association).

🐾 **Put some distance between your dog and their trigger**

Sometimes calmly crossing the road or moving in another direction to put more distance between your dog and his trigger *before* he reacts will be enough.

🐾 **Distract him, using a treat, ball or toy – learn 'look at me'**

Sometimes moving away before a trigger approaches is not always possible, so to help prevent your dog from reacting (which is always our goal) you can distract them quickly by using a treat, squeaky toy or ball (or whatever it is he loves most) to get their attention. Even more useful is to teach them 'look at me' (*see* p. 113).

🐾 **Reward no reaction**

If they do take a look over and don't react then be sure to mark this behaviour with a 'yes', create some distance between them and the trigger (which provides a functional reward) and then praise or give them a treat as a bonus reward to really reinforce that desired behaviour.

DO NOT reward aggressive reactions

If your dog has started to react you must distract them enough to stop the barking or growling <u>before</u> removing them, otherwise they think their barking/growling worked to remove the threat. Try making a strange noise if you don't have a toy or haven't trained the 'look at me' distraction. If they have reacted aggressively, take them straight home so they start to learn that an aggressive response means the fun ends.

'LOOK AT ME' TECHNIQUE

This is a distraction technique which can be used both in stressful situations and as part of obedience training. Practise at home with no distractions.

1. Use something to get their attention – a treat, toy or ball.

2. Bring the reward up to your eye level.

3. When their eyes lock with yours, say 'yes' to mark the desired response (looking at you) and <u>immediately</u> give them the reward.

4. Once they are reliably looking at you each time you try to get their attention, introduce the cue words 'look at me'.

5. If you don't have a treat, toy or ball, the cue words can be used to get your dog's attention and you can reward them with a pat or say 'good boy'.

It is important to walk away calmly, if you have used this technique in a stressful situation.

See p. 151 for how to condition the word 'yes' as a reinforcer.

How to introduce people to your dog

If your dog is very nervous or reacts to people inappropriately, it is important you don't introduce them to too many people, too quickly. Ideally you'd only bring a new person into your home once or twice a week at the most and your aim is to create a calm, positive experience every time.

1. Put your dog on a leash and using a treat, toy or ball, have the other person slowly come into the house or room with the reward easily visible.

2. If your dog moves towards them to investigate they should offer your dog the reward and speak in a low, calm and encouraging voice. Having your visitor give your dog his reward will help create the positive association we are after.

3. If your dog displays any signs of anxiety or aggression, use distraction to divert their attention and your visitor should stop and calmly back away, increasing the distance between themselves and the dog.

4. You might both sit down at a safe distance from your dog and ignore him, all the while your guest can hold the reward in sight. If ignored, dogs will sometimes get curious and slowly make their way over to investigate, or once your dog is calm your visitor could offer a 'good dog' and reward.

5. Never push the issue, force your dog to go over or tell him off as it can create further anxiety and a negative association with that person or other people in general.

TIP: Always ensure people take off sunglasses, hats or hoodies, avoid carrying bags or other items your dog might react to, and make no sudden movements towards you or the dog.

Take your dog out to observe other dogs

Dog parks or beaches are often not recommended by dog trainers in general due to the large number of dogs and people in a small contained space, let alone for dogs that have poor social skills, are fearful or aggressive. However, if it is your only option to let your dog run off-lead and really exert themselves physically (which can be more important for some breeds than others), then introduce this environment to them in a slow and controlled manner. You have to of course make sure their recall is bullet proof too! (*See* p. 125 for more information on recall.)

Start by simply going to the park but don't go inside, instead allow your dog to watch and observe the other dogs and how they are interacting from a safe distance and where they are not going to react.

When another dog comes near the fence, give your dog a treat (or play with the toy or ball depending on their preferences) to help create a positive association with other dogs.

Apply similar techniques as outlined in walking a nervous or aggressive dog, such as going at times when it is quieter, starting far away and slowly moving closer. This is where getting professional help is important as you want to do this in a way that your dog is not pushed too far, too fast and starts to react.

Re-training older dogs

The following are very important when re-training an older dog, but apply to training any dog.

- Be clear and consistent with your responses and techniques

- Don't give up in frustration too early. Understand that the process is going to be slow, so be patient, use repetition and create positive associations with new experiences and triggers.

- Don't reinforce the poor behaviour, which creates confusion in your dog and can lead to more anxiety or unwanted behaviour

- If you are trying to improve behaviour issues with an older dog it is important that you remain calm and are firm but fair, to provide them with the good solid leadership that dogs need

- Create a calm, loving environment around them to help overcome their fears so that you can build their confidence and interactions with other dogs and people, and they can become a happy, well-balanced dog that loves to embrace play.

There are plenty of videos and articles in the Training & Behaviour section of poochesatplay.com to help you identify and treat anxiety or other unwanted behaviours.

CALMNESS, CONSISTENCY AND PATIENCE ARE KEY

SIGNS OF ANXIETY AND FEAR

If a dog is anxious or fearful in a social situation the signs to look out for can range from the very subtle to the downright obvious. They can react in two different ways – a dog might appear either submissive or threatening. Either way, you need to pay attention to what your dog's body language is telling you so that you can remove them from a situation where they, or another dog, are not comfortable.

Submissive – appeasing signs of fear or anxiety

Signs to look for:

- Constant licking of the lips, flicking the tongue rapidly or a yawn which can indicate stress and anxiety

- They might shy away or turn their head, fold their ears back, tuck their tail under their body, or lower their head or body in a cowering position

- Their eyes may show more white than usual, known as 'whale eye', or they might avert their gaze

- A nervous puppy or a dog may roll over onto their back or side to expose their tummy (often accompanied with the head or eyes turned away) or emit a sprinkle of urine, which is a very passive, submissive response

- Muzzle licking is something I've noticed that Darcy does, particularly with big dogs he wants to get to know but is a little wary of. This indicates he wants attention (of course he does ... he loves being the centre of attention!) and he usually does it when he is greeting the other dog

- Your dog may try to divert attention away from themselves or calm themselves down by sniffing the area around them, sneezing, shaking or shaking themselves off, pacing and spinning

ROLLS ONTO BACK EXPOSING STOMACH AND THROAT

HEAD TURNS TO AVOID DIRECT EYE CONTACT

BODY LOWERED

EARS BACK

TAIL DOWN

Defensive – aggressive response to fear

Just because your dog is acting out aggressively, it doesn't mean that they are a mean, nasty dog that is trying to start a fight. Dogs use defensive, aggressive signals to warn a perceived threat to go away or to create distance between them and something they think is dangerous. This needs to be interpreted and handled correctly to avoid the fear being reinforced, or someone being bitten. *See* pp. 112–113 on walking a nervous or aggressive dog.

I TOUCH MORE ON FEAR-BASED AGGRESSION IN PP. 123–124

Signs to look for:

- The usual indicators of an anxious dog such as the ears back, tail tucked, body lowered etc.

- A lip drawn back or even curled slightly to show some teeth

- Dilated pupils

- The hair on their back (known as hackles) rising

- Maybe even a growl before they bark or lash out

TAIL TUCKED

EARS BACK

NOSE WRINKLED

LIPS SLIGHTLY CURLED (TEETH MAY BE VISIBLE)

Offensive aggression

If your dog is put in a situation where he feels he is left with no other option, and he feels confident, his body language will be a lot more assertive.

Signs to look out for:

- 🐾 A stiff-legged stance with their body and ears forward

- 🐾 A stiff tail

- 🐾 Hackles raised

- 🐾 Mouth open and teeth showing

- 🐾 Threatening facial expression.

THESE ARE SIGNS WE DO NOT WANT TO SEE IN A DOG

TAIL RAISED AND BRISTLED

EARS FORWARD (MAY BE SPREAD SLIGHTLY TO FORM A v)

LIPS CURLED AND TEETH VISIBLE

Tail wagging

You may think that a dog wagging its tail is a good sign. This is not always the case.

There is a lot of storytelling going on if you take the time to read a dog's tail. I can tell when Darcy has spotted his favourite toy or ball in the distance and is thinking about play before he has even made a move for it. His tail is the giveaway as it starts to make this cute little movement that seems to mimic the cogs in his brain as they start to spin. I only have to look around to see what has caught his attention (which he knows I am going to do next as he's caught my attention with his tail wag!), and he is off and running. It makes me laugh every time how well he has spoken to me without saying a word.

How high or low the tail is held can tell us a lot about how the dog is feeling. An anxious dog will have its tail tucked low and in between its legs, whereas a confident or aggressive dog will hold its tail erect. The tail on a relaxed dog is going to be somewhere in the middle. The lower down it is being held, the less secure and more anxious a dog is feeling, and the higher up it moves the more alert the dog is becoming, which may then escalate into a threatening vertical position.

You need to consider where your dog's tail sits naturally when it is relaxed (as different breeds have tails that sit at different heights), to make a read on how high or low it is. It can be particularly hard for dogs with docked tails as they can't signal how they are feeling, while other dogs or people can be unsure on how to read them which may lead to some warning signs being ignored.

RELAXED

The relaxed dog with a neutral tail might also give a gentle wag with a tentative hello, or a broader relaxed wag that says I'm pretty pleased right about now.

HAPPY

There's the very excited and happy 'I'm all in' wagging tail from side to side or round in circles, that might even have the back end join in with a wiggle.

AFRAID

Then there's the lower, slow tail wag of a dog that's not quite sure yet, to the tail tucked between the legs (which you now know indicates fear or anxiety).

AROUSED

The one that you don't want to get wrong is the tail held rigid and high that is moving almost vibration like. This is the one that may not be a friendly gesture but rather one of threat, even though it might be seen to be 'wagging'.

UNDERSTANDING FEAR-BASED AGGRESSION

Aggressive behaviour in dogs is often a fear-based response and is widely misunderstood (and mistreated). Sometimes they are just highly excited.

Reasons for aggressive behaviour include:

🐾 A lack of socialisation

🐾 Past traumatic experiences which sees them responding to a trigger that they consider to be a perceived threat

🐾 Poor or forceful training methods that leads to a dog either shutting down entirely or coming out all guns blazing when faced with a fearful situation

🐾 Genetic factors such as poor breeding can play a role, but there is still too much of a misconception that breed alone creates an aggressive dog

🐾 A painful medical condition that has gone undetected, so if there is a sudden behaviour change in your dog, it is important as a first step to get a medical check to rule out any sickness or injury that may be causing them to act out

NEVER PUT YUR FACE UP CLOSE TO A DOG'S FACE

The lack of socialisation in dogs can cause a dog to appear to suddenly lash out and is usually very successful for them as the other dog or person moves away from them, or you move your dog away from the situation. This provides strong reinforcement for your dog and tells them that their aggressive behaviour works, as it is successful at moving them or the threat away. So, the next time they are feeling threatened they will choose to do exactly the same behaviour. Why wouldn't they? It works really well. As a result the barking, lunging and biting continues with more intensity and frequency.

While the most obvious answer is to not put your dog in a situation where it feels threatened, this is not always possible (except in the example of kids and dogs mentioned to the right ... please stop doing that people), so you can use the distraction example talked about earlier.

It's important to know that simply distracting your dog is not addressing the underlying fear causing the reaction, it is just a tool to manage a stressful situation. The long-term solution is to counter-condition and/or desensitise them to the trigger. There is a video on poochesatplay.com featuring Tikka the Staffordshire terrier that shows how this is done, as well as other videos and articles on dog reactivity and aggression. In the case of severe reactivity or aggression however I would suggest you enlist the help of a very experienced trainer that uses positive reinforcement techniques.

REMEMBER
A dog's discomfort builds up to a point where the dog is no longer able to contain their response and lashes out as it tries to remove the threat.

You only have to watch the many videos on YouTube or Facebook where toddlers are riding on the backs of dogs, pulling their ears or tails, or the dog is put in situations that are often deemed funny or cute to see some classic examples of fear-based aggression. Next time you see one of these videos, see if you can notice any of those subtle signs mentioned on pp. 117–122 to recognise that the dog certainly doesn't think that it is funny or cute. It is often only a matter of time before the dog snaps!

RECALL

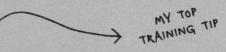

MY TOP
TRAINING TIP

Being able to stop your dog when they are running off and call them back to you is one of the most important obedience exercises you can teach them. If you have not done any obedience training to understand the process behind recall, then I strongly suggest you attend an obedience class or seek the help of a trainer.

If your dog isn't reliable with their recall always take along some treats (or whatever they are most motivated by as a reward) and ensure they know you have them before letting them wander off (assuming it's a gated area).

THE STEPS OF RECALL

1. Call their name

2. When they look at you say, 'yes, good boy'

3. Give them the cue by saying 'come'

4. Move backwards (gathering up the lead if you are still teaching them and using a lead to guide them)

5. When they come directly to you, reward with treat or praise etc. (or you could lure them into a sit with a treat and give it to them when they do)

SLOWLY BUILD UP THE DISTRACTION AND DISTANCE

- 🐾 Start practising at home keeping your dog on his lead with few distractions. Use treats so that you can either lure them back towards you, or you can gently guide them back with the lead

- 🐾 Increase the distance and distraction until you are off-lead at home

- 🐾 Start the process again out front of your house (gates closed)

- 🐾 Increase the distraction by moving to the park at quiet times, then slowly introduce more distraction and distance at busier times until you can confidently let them off in a park with fencing and so on

Where people go wrong with recall

LEAVE THE PARK EVERY TIME YOU CALL THEM BACK

Make sure you call your dog back to you at the park and reward their return, then allow them to go off and play again. Don't stick to the same number of times you call and release them either otherwise they'll catch on. You want to keep them coming back in anticipation of good things, rather than associate a recall with end of play every time.

THE REWARD FOR RETURNING ISN'T ENTICING ENOUGH

Dogs do things to better their situation, so we need to be far more interesting and exciting than anything else that is going on. The key to developing an effective recall is understanding what motivates your dog. Take a few different levels of reward with you if you struggle to get your dog's attention. While my dog Darcy is great at recall, food is not a big motivator for him, so to lure him over with the promise of a treat when

he's in the middle of having a great play is pointless. However, if I was in the distance and he heard the squeak of his rubber chicken, he'd be back quicker than flash-lightening, even if it was his best mate he was in the midst of playing with.

INADVERTENTLY TEACHING YOUR DOG TO IGNORE YOU

If you are standing on the other side of the park and keep calling out your dog's name and they don't respond, you are giving them the chance to pretend they didn't hear or see you. Never allow your dog to keep ignoring you. If you do, you are teaching your dog it is ok to ignore you. If you are not confident about their recall, then you should always make sure you are close enough to entice them with a treat and an exuberant call.

DON'T PUNISH YOUR DOG WHEN THEY FINALLY RETURN

By punishing your dog when they do finally return, they will associate the punishment with their return. So next time you call them they will be less likely to return because they don't want to be punished again. It is up to you to ensure you don't put yourself or your dog in the position of ignoring you all of those times.

Of course you don't need to praise their slow wander over if they do usually have a good recall. Instead, give them an alternative command, such as a 'sit' and reward them sitting before putting them on lead and calmly taking them home.

OTHER TIPS

Tie a 1–2 metre (yard) of ribbon on their collar when you first move them off-lead and into public areas so that they can still run around freely. The ribbon will give you something to grab on to and pull them in to you as you call their name.

If your dog is a beagle, labrador or other dog that has a strong scent drive, you are pushing your luck trying to call them back when they have their nose stuck to the ground following a trail. Wait until they are distracted from the task that they are zeroed in on, so they are more likely to focus on the reward on offer. This also applies when your dog is mid-play; wait until the moment the dogs have taken a break from playing and that is when you should time your call.

Major problems with recall can't be left for too long and expected to somehow fix themselves, so seek the services of a qualified and experienced trainer. You can visit poochesatplay.com for my video example and other useful dog training tips.

DOG ETIQUETTE IN PUBLIC SPACES

Dog beaches and parks tend to have an increased risk of dog attacks and accidents. Here are some tips to keep in mind to help when you are heading to a dog beach or park with your pooch.

GOOD SIGNS TO LOOK FOR

- A play bow from one dog to another inviting play
- A tag and run request. Not to be confused with a dog coming up to nip at your dog, but rather when dogs are interacting nicely and one bounces up to give a bit of a tag then runs away inviting your dog to chase. If your dog shies away or growls, then they are clearly not up for the invitation, so try to block the other dog from any further attempts or ask the owner nicely to just keep them away as your dog is feeling a little unsure or anxious. (Or not so nicely if they don't get the message!)
- Mimicking each other's behaviour. Good, fair dog play is when each dog takes turns winning and losing. Even if the dogs like to jump all over each other, mouth or nip, as long as they are taking turns and taking some time out then this is okay. Just make sure their adrenaline doesn't start to rise too much and they start getting over excited as that can quickly lead to a spat. If things start getting a bit out of control, call them off to take some time out.

- Remember, if play has gotten a bit rough or one gives a yelp, don't panic and pick them up. Usually the other will stop and you'll see one of those time-out signals I discussed on p. 105 such as a shake

WHAT TO WATCH OUT FOR

- One dog is constantly on top of the other or dominating the play, rather than taking turns
- A larger dog nipping or grabbing at a smaller dog or puppy's neck, legs or body
- I'm extra watchful when two very strong dog breeds that aren't regular play buddies, play too rough or bite too much. Even if in play, as it may quickly escalate
- Watch the play between a number of dogs carefully because if one starts to feel threatened or anxious and acts out aggressively to protect itself, you want to be able to quickly remove all dogs calmly from the situation
- One dog is constantly chasing another and nipping at their heels. (This is different to a tag and chase as described above.) You might see this with working dogs chasing smaller dogs around the park, so you need to ensure it doesn't start to get intimidating for the dog being chased, which can lead them to snap back
- One dog pouncing on another for a game of wrestle when the other dog is not looking, is uncomfortable and showing signs of stress, or is old or injured
- Mounting, aka humping. There are many reasons why dogs mount others and it isn't always dominance or sexual. However, it isn't great manners or can hurt another dog and set off a reaction
- Be extra careful if there are small and large dogs playing together as the risk can be much higher

Children at the dog beach or park

If you take both your dog and children along to a dog beach or park it's important that children don't run around because it will invite a dog to jump and chase them. If a dog is running at them, they should turn their back and fold their arms. A good firm 'no' can also help, along with quick intervention from an adult or the dog's owner. Please tell them not to run away screaming as the dog will think this is a great invitation to play and it will make matters worse.

Avoid confrontations – keep yourself and your dog moving

- Watch your dog at all times when at a dog beach or park

- Don't stand around chatting, keep you and your dog moving

- If you do see a dog fight, don't rush in to grab your dog by the collar as you could be bitten

- Stop a dog fight with a loud and assertive 'stop', make a loud noise, or throw a lead or some water in between the dogs to break their attention

- Both owners should put their dogs immediately on lead and move them far enough away from each other so that they are not reacting, but ideally you will let them calm down in front of one another so that it finishes on a calm, positive note to avoid reinforcing any fear from future interactions

REMEMBER
You should be able to stop your dog in their chase and call them back to you. A foolproof recall is something every dog owner should have down pat as early as possible for the safety of all dogs and people. *See pp. 125–126* for my training tip to help you and your dog with recall.

Be mindful of your own dog's behaviour

There is nothing worse than the owner that let's their dog run wild with no thought for how other dogs or owners might be feeling. We've all been there when a large, bounding dog makes a beeline for us or our dog and the owner shouts out 'don't worry they just want to play'.

If you have a dog that is reactive then you know this is a recipe for disaster. If this happens to me with Darcy and it is a much larger dog (which he can react to if rushed at) or I am unsure of the other dog's intentions, I don't panic and pick him up, I simply call him 'close', step in front of him calmly and make myself look big or unwelcoming so that usually the other dog stops in its tracks and rethinks its approach. If they are indeed friendly and just want to say hello, once they have stopped I might then calmly call them over and invite the introduction, after a quick check that Darcy is indeed okay with that. (Usually he is, unless it is a german shepherd ... he clearly had a lack of socialisation or a bad experience in the past with one which is something we are currently working on.)

If the other dog still bounds up I usually yell out to their owner that my dog is NOT okay with other dogs (they don't need to know he usually is) which generally provokes the owner to take action. I then might have a word with them about the need to be a little more mindful about how other dogs might be feeling and not assume everything is okay for the safety of everyone.

Likewise, if your dog tends to play too rough, mount other dogs or displays other bad manners, then you really do need to be more aware of your own behaviour and the responsibility you have as a dog owner, and start working on your own dog's socialisation skills again.

HOW AND WHEN TO APPROACH A DOG

You or your child may be compelled to pat a dog that looks perfectly friendly or in need of a cuddle, but you may be doing more harm than good. A dog who is tied up or on-lead may feel they have no way to control the situation or escape a perceived threat, so you may inadvertently frighten them.

TIPS FOR GREETING A DOG

🐾 Even if you ask an owner walking with their dog if you can pat their dog and they say yes, always invite the dog to say hi to you first. Be mindful that the owner may not be good at reading their own dog's body language

🐾 To invite the dog over, turn your side to them, pat your leg and encourage them to come over to you. If the dog doesn't approach or moves away, leave them alone!

🐾 If the dog reluctantly comes over displaying any of those subtle signs of fear or anxiety (tail tucked, yawning, tongue flicking, panting, ducking or dropping its head, averting the eye etc.), then give them back their space by increasing your distance

🐾 If the dog does happily come over, then gently give them a tickle under the chin, slowly coming in from in front or underneath their face, not over the top. Dogs interpret gestures differently to us, so avoid bending over to greet or stroke them on the head

- Keep your face a safe distance away. Whilst they may not mean to, they might get a bit excited, and jump up and accidentally connect with your face. I've made this mistake myself with a puppy and wore some little teeth marks on my nose for about a week. Or, if you were to do this to a dog like Darcy, who is very happy to meet new friends, you would likely get his eager tongue licking the inside of your mouth if he can get to it. (Disgusting I know, but he has managed to kiss many a person who chose to ignore my warnings of an impending kiss and kept going anyway ... eww)

- If you see a dog tied up and its owner is not around, just leave it alone. Humans aren't great at reading each other's body language, and when it comes to a dog we're even less so. It's best to err on the side of caution with a dog, because at least a person is much less likely to bite you if you encroach on their personal space

- We all have our bad days ... and so can dogs. Even your own dog or those who you may have patted before can not want to be touched, so always keep an eye on their body language and what the dog is really saying to you. Avoid hugging them or kissing them on the nose – anything that gets too much in their space and might make them feel uncomfortable

WHY DOGS NEED EXERCISE

In the wild, dogs would spend their days hunting for food with their pack and most certainly weren't left alone all day like many dogs are these days. This is why we see so many dog behaviour problems and anxiety in our modern-day dogs.

IT MAKES DOGS FEEL GOOD

When dogs exercise, their brains produce and release the same endorphins that make them feel happy and energetic as we humans do. So exercise improves their physical and mental wellbeing in much the same way as it does for us.

IT CAN HELP KEEP BEHAVIOUR ISSUES AT BAY

Without adequate exercise, dogs become bored and frustrated, leading to destructive and unwanted behaviours including barking, whining, digging, chewing, aggression, escaping the house and more. The most common dog behaviour issues trainers and vets deal with are often caused by a lack of physical exercise and mental stimulation. Anxiety, sadness or depression can be exacerbated if dogs aren't given the chance to be exposed to the world outside their home. Exercise also helps strengthen your bond with your dog which can also help with obedience training and keep problem behaviours at bay.

IT IS VITAL FOR GOOD HEALTH

Exercise promotes new cell growth and blood circulation within their stomachs and intestines to help stimulate urination and bowel movements. If pets aren't exercising enough they can lose muscle mass and gain weight as they are not burning off the calories they are taking in each day. Their joints can also become stiff which can make conditions like arthritis worse.

How much exercise does your dog need?

ALL DOGS NEED BETWEEN 30 MINUTES AND 2 HOURS EXERCISE EVERY DAY, NOT JUST WEEKENDS!

Sporting/herding dogs are going to need a lot more than a bulldog, but too many owners of small breeds like chihuahuas and poodles think they don't need proper exercise. Breeds such as bulldogs and pugs will put on weight because they are often kept as indoor dogs and do not receive enough exercise, not to mention the pug's love of food! Only the other day, I had someone say to me that they were looking for a small dog as a pet because small dogs don't need to be walked every day. I'm not sure why this is such a commonly held belief, but it is certainly not true.

Some flat-faced brachycephalic breeds like bulldogs don't tolerate a lot of daily physical exercise, particularly if it is a warm day, but they still need to be kept moving. Games, such as fetch or tug-of-war played several times a day at home will help prevent weight gain and keep such dogs mentally stimulated.

Senior dogs

If you don't use it, you lose it, as the old saying goes, for us and our dog. Older dogs, even those with conditions such as arthritis, need to keep their joints moving. If you aren't sure how much exercise your older dog needs, talk to your veterinarian about pain medication and other pet health treatments that can help reduce inflammation, as well as natural alternatives and supplements.

Puppies – start slowly

Over-exercising your puppy can damage its developing joints, causing damage such as early arthritis, so they need much less exercise than fully grown dogs. Also think about where and how you are exercising your puppy – long walks on hard pavement or roads will have more impact on their joints than taking them to a local grassy park or beach.

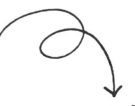

DON'T OVER-EXERCISE YOUR PUPPY

The American Kennel Club suggests a ratio of five minutes exercise per month of age, up to twice a day, until the puppy is fully grown. For example, 15 minutes up to twice a day when they are three months old, 20 minutes when four months old etc. Remember, larger breed dogs take longer to become an adult, so take this into consideration as well.

You can burn off puppies' excess energy at home with gentle games of tug-of-war (and redirect some of their need to chew with this too!), hide-and-seek, or use interactive toys and puzzles to get their brains working along with their bodies. Time spent in the yard at home, no matter how big, is no substitute for exploring new environments and socialising with other dogs.

But it's raining (and other excuses!)

There is simply no excuse for not exercising your dog. If you are physically unable to walk your dog then seek the services of a local dog walker, ask a friend, family member or neighbour to assist you, or see if they know of a local student that is eager for some extra pocket money and wishes they had a dog of their own, to walk your dog for you.

There are also many websites popping up all over the world where people offer their services for pet walking at low cost and dog walking businesses galore.

NO EXCUSES!

IT'S IMPORTANT!

LET YOUR DOG HAVE A SNIFF

A dog's sense of smell is its most important sense and our dogs absorb the world around them through their nose. Trees and fire hydrants are often referred to as the local community notice board, as many dogs leave their story behind for another to read all about them.

The higher up the better, particularly for male dogs, as it can take longer for their scent to be washed away by others and also sends out a message about their height, 'I'm the big dog around this 'hood'.

Then there is the dog version of the human handshake and 'how are you' upon greeting. Yes, I'm referring to the good old rear end circle dance when two dogs meet. Every dog has their own signature scent and it is believed that from this they can tell all the information they need to know about another dog, from its age, gender, sexual status, overall health and even their emotional state, from the pheromones in their urine as well as the glands around their private parts.

It's a bit of a ritual when dogs meet for them to touch noses with other non-threatening animals they wish to make friends with, sniff mouths and then beeline for the backside. Darcy is a very inquisitive dog and is always first in. He'll even get up on his hind legs to get as close as possible to a big dog's behind to get a good whiff and has no shame when it comes to sticking his head in as close as possible as a dog pees, which can be somewhat embarrassing, not to mention messy if he gets in too close!

Dogs can also read a lot of information about us by smelling around our 'bits', which is why you may have encountered a snout or two in your crotch before.

They can tell which other people, dogs or animals have been somewhere before them, scent weather changes and some well-honed noses can sniff out anything they are trained to detect from bombs to termites, and cancer to drugs.

LOOKING AFTER YOUR DOG'S MENTAL WELLBEING

Mental stimulation is just as important as physical exercise for our dogs. You can help keep your dog's brain stimulated in many ways by taking them on new routes, different dog parks, or introducing new dog toys, games and activities to your routine.

Many common problems with dog behaviour can be managed by developing a full environmental enrichment plan to ensure your dog has everything they need to keep their bodies and brains active.

SOME SIGNS TO WATCH FOR

🐾 Destructive behaviour including digging and chewing

🐾 Barking and whining

🐾 Weight gain is a sign that your pet needs more exercise, but make sure you aren't overfeeding them as well

🐾 Your dog is hyperactive or difficult to control on walks because they've got too much pent-up energy or aren't used to being out and about. I can often tell when a dog isn't walked much by their behaviour on-lead. They can calm down pretty quickly once they start getting the appropriate exercise.

🐾 Repeated escapes from home

🐾 Pacing the room and not sitting still

🐾 Signs of withdrawal, anxiety or depression-like symptoms. Definitely get these checked by a vet as they might be caused by other issues including pain

ADULT DOGS NEED TO EXERCISE AT LEAST 30 MINUTES EVERY DAY!

It is up to you to try to understand what your dog is trying to communicate to you through their behaviour and to see where you may be letting them down. (Sorry but in most cases it does come back to us!).

Dogs that suffer from anxiety or other Separation Related Behaviour (SRB) tend to display the behaviour immediately or not long after your departure, while a dog that starts with barking or digging later in the day generally indicates boredom.

TOP TIPS TO BEAT THE HOME-ALONE BLUES

❂ ENSURE THEY GET THEIR DAILY WALK

A tired dog is a good dog. Ensure your dog gets a morning walk, even just that all-so-important ten-minute chance to sniff around outside before you leave them alone all day and take them out again when you get home. Hire someone to walk them during the day or share hosting of doggy dates with a friend or neighbour if your dogs get along well.

❂ DON'T WASTE FEEDING TIME WITH A BOWL

If you feed your dog kibble, then throw or hide it around the yard or rooms of your house and encourage them to seek it out. Hunting for their food mimics how dogs in the wild foraged for their food and helps keep them mentally and physically stimulated.

If you feed your dog a wet or raw food, you obviously need to be mindful of health and hygiene issues. Probably best for those that have mastered the Treasure Hunt game (*see* p. 156) and are highly motivated for food, so that you don't risk it sitting out in the heat too long. Inside or out you could place wet/raw food on saucers to reduce contamination. Of course do read all of the health and safety considerations of raw feeding, especially for immune compromised animals and humans, on p. 41.

❂ PROVIDE TWO DIFFERENT TYPES OF INTERACTIVE TOYS

Interactive toys encourage dogs to use their body and mind to work the treat, kibble or meat out of the toy and mimic how they hunt and forage for food in the wild.

Think about what type of toy would suit your dog the best. Some nervous dogs may need a quiet soft interactive toy that doesn't make loud noises when rolling around on floorboards, while other dogs may go crazy for the sound of a rattling marble or bell inside a treat dispensing toy as it rolls along.

Toys like the Kong Wobbler stuffed with their wet food or mince works well, whilst freezing it can keep them occupied for hours and is great for the warmer weather too.

Another option for the warmer months is to simply place some treats or meat in a container, fill it with water or use a bone broth instead and freeze it. Also add in a combination of a rolling or hanging treat dispensing toy if it is going to be a long day so that they have a couple of options to keep them occupied.

🐾 INSTALL A SANDPIT

ESPECIALLY GREAT FOR DOGS THAT LIKE TO DIG

Some dogs just love to dig, but if it becomes a problem there may be another underlying problem. Start by checking they have enough shade from the elements, as in the warmer weather in particular they may actually be digging a hole to lie in and cool themselves down. If it is because they are bored or anxious and/or it makes them feel good, then you can use a sandpit to divert the digging to a designated area and bury treats or toys to encourage them to dig their heart out. This is another great way to mimic how a dog might forage for its food in the wild and helps work their bodies and their brains.

🐾 GIVE THEM A SAFE, CALMING SPACE TO RETIRE TO

If you have followed the tips above, then quite frankly your dog should have worn itself out and be more than happy to sleep the afternoon away until you come home. Ensure your dog has a room indoors or, if left outdoors, a sturdy kennel with bedding and plenty of protection from the elements that they can retreat to and relax. If your dog is reactive to outside noises or has a bit of anxiety, then some studies have found that playing some soft calming music can help, whilst indoor dogs might do well with some DogTV (yes there is such a thing). Music can also help block out noises too if they have noise phobia or are a reactive barker.

🐾 HUMAN CONTACT

Dogs need human companionship. They're pack animals and are not designed to be left alone all day or out in the backyard with little interaction with their family. The company of another pet is not always enough either. Just like us humans, dogs don't necessarily like every dog they meet, or even if they do they may not play together when left alone, so getting another dog is generally not a solution to addressing your dog's boredom or anxiety. You can often also end up with two dogs on your hands who are exhibiting problem behaviour.

🐾 FAMILY TIME

Life can be lonely for dogs that are kept exclusively outdoors, away from their pack. If allowing them inside your home to join the family is not an option, at least some of the time, it is imperative that their family spends a lot of time outside playing with them. Playing games requiring exercise, such as tug-of-war, fetching balls, frisbee etc., are great. Your dog actually *needs* to be with you because, to him, you are his pack, so ideally it is important to let your dog inside with you as regularly as possible.

If you are adamant they are not allowed inside, then bring their kennel as close to the family living area as possible so that they can still see you and feel close enough to protect you (which is something else they *need* to do).

OBEDIENCE TRAINING

Obedience training helps to build trust and mutual respect, offers mental and physical stimulation, helps your pet understand right and wrong, and, as pack animals, provides your dog with the leadership they need to help reduce stress and confusion in an uncertain world.

Basic commands all dogs should know include: sit, come, drop, leave it, stay, wait, stop, no and quiet. 'Look at me' (*see* p. 113) is also very useful for bringing your dog's focus back to you and is one I use on Darcy quite a bit to distract or disrupt him from reacting to a potential trigger.

These key commands help to keep your dog safe and make it easier for you to keep him under control in public places or dangerous situations.

Helps address problem behaviours

If your dog is well-trained, with good manners, he will be more manageable, relaxed, content and confident. Most of the problem behaviours dog trainers see are not because a dog intentionally sets out to do the wrong thing. The dogs are usually unsure, frightened, stressed or frustrated by different situations.

If their leader (you) is not stepping up to the plate and taking control of a scary situation, they may feel they have no choice but to take matters into their own hands and this is where we see dogs acting out.

Obedience training also allows you to give your dog an alternative command such as 'Sit' or 'On your mat' to help prevent or control unwanted behaviours. For example, by teaching your dog to sit when you enter a room and rewarding this behaviour, this response is strengthened and is more likely to occur in the future. Likewise you can use obedience training to prevent your dog from jumping up or barking when someone comes to the front door by having them go to their bed or sit and wait until they are given permission to say hello.

Obedience training also helps you to provide clear and consistent boundaries for your dog. Dogs respond best to structure and routine.

Golden rules of obedience training

TIMING IS CRUCIAL

Dogs can only make a connection between a behaviour (their action) and a consequence (good or bad) if the consequence/reward is given at the time they are displaying that action or within a couple of seconds.

This is just one of the many reasons why you should never reprimand your dog when you get home for doing something such as toileting or digging during the day when you weren't there. They will not understand why they are in trouble as the event has been long forgotten. Too often owners believe their dog is feeling guilt in these instances, when in fact your dog is simply reacting to your response and body language.

TRAINING NEEDS TO BE FUN FOR BOTH OF YOU

If your dog is not into treats, then find out what else motivates them to do what you need them to do. This could be a ball, a game of tug, pats or praise. Every dog has *something* that will motivate them, it's up to you to find out what this is and know that this can change as well. One day it might be treats, the next a toy. Just like us they can change their mind based on how they are feeling on the day.

TRAIN IN A CALM, SAFE, DISTRACTION-FREE ENVIRONMENT

Dogs can't learn anything if they are anxious or stressed, so keep the distractions to a minimum, make sure they are in a space they feel comfortable in with no triggers around and use positive reinforcement to reward desired behaviour.

BE CONSISTENT

You always need to be *clear* with your command, *concise* (short, one-word cues) and *consistent*. This means you and everyone in the household has to use the same set of rules, give the same command for the same action and don't set the dog up to fail by not being consistent with your commands or boundaries.

USE POSITIVE REINFORCEMENT

Dogs learn best through positive reinforcement, rewarding the behaviours we want from them at the time they are displaying them. If you yell at your dog, you can reinforce an unwanted behaviour without realising it. For example, if your dog jumps up on you because he wants your attention he is getting exactly that, even if you yell at them to 'get down' or push them down.

Focusing on positive reinforcement and rewarding your dog for desired behaviour is the way to go. If we use jumping for example, this would be ignoring them and turning your back on your dog when they are trying to jump up to get your attention or say hello, and the moment all four of their legs are back on the ground that is when you give them the attention, praise or a pat. Or if they have a reliable sit, walk in the door and before they have the chance to jump say 'sit' and reward that when they do. If you are consistent with this soon you will find your dog sitting and waiting in eager anticipation when you walk in the door.

Darcy was always running to the front door and jumping up on my legs whenever I entered the house until I taught him 'on your bed', which is in the lounge room and close to the front door. Often I can see him through the window running to the front door, then stopping in his tracks as he remembers what to do and racing back to his bed quivering in excitement for me to enter. Sometimes he still forgets in his excitement, so before he has managed to jump up on me I point or simply say 'on your bed' and off he bolts. I always reward that, but he gets extra high praise and a tummy rub when he has already placed himself there and is waiting for me to go to him without any cue, as that is the desired behaviour I really want.

How to condition a 'reinforcer'

Using a verbal conditioned reinforcer such as 'yes' or 'good dog', or a training clicker helps you to 'mark' your dog's correct behaviour and helps them understand exactly when they have done what you want. It's all in the timing and you have to condition your dog to the reinforcer first. To do this you can use a treat, toy, game of tug, pat, or praise – whatever motivates them most – as a reward.

In the very early stages you don't need them to be doing anything for the reward, you simply say the word 'yes' or press the clicker and immediately give them the reward. This must be within 0.5–1 second and no more than 3 seconds. Use a different voice or tone when you use a verbal reinforcer.

Practise this a few times every day until you are confident they understand that the sound equals a reward. It is important every time you say 'yes' or use the clicker, it is immediately followed by the reward while you are still in this teaching phase.

Start to use the clicker or say 'yes' when your dog is distracted, until they are reliably turning to look at you as soon as they hear it and come for their reward. Puppies can be conditioned to a reinforcer in just a few attempts, while some older dogs may take longer, so only move into the next phase when they are ready.

Once you have fully conditioned the reinforcer you can use it to mark desired behaviour in a training scenario. *See* pp. 156–162 for some examples in the games and tricks pages.

Phasing out continuous rewards

Move to an irregular pattern of reinforcement with the reward when your dog responds correctly 90% of the time. Only reward those attempts that are faster and more accurate to encourage them to do better. Some dogs are really motivated by training and/or the promise of a treat so will keep striving to outdo their last attempt, while others might need some verbal encouragement when they do it right, but only use their favourite reward for when they do really well.

Never stop rewarding completely – even the most well-behaved dog needs reminding that they'll get a reward when they do what you ask or do particularly well. If you stop altogether they may lose interest, get confused and start to devalue the conditioned reinforcer.

WHEN TRAINING MULTIPLE DOGS

- You need to train one dog at a time

- Don't lock one dog in a separate room as they may bark and whine, causing a distraction

- Leave one in the yard with a raw meaty bone (remember to read the safety section on bones on pp. 70–72 first, of course) and train indoors with the other dog, then swap around

- Ask a family member to take one dog for a walk while you train the other at home, then you take turns

- Of course, the hide-and-seek game can be done with multiple dogs, as can the treasure hunt if your dogs definitely don't have any food resource guarding issues

DOG SPORTING ACTIVITIES

Working dogs, such as border collies, kelpies and cattle dogs (Australian working breeds), Australian and German shepherds, Belgian malinois, huskies and many others were bred to do a job, so being confined to a yard in suburbia often leads to many problem behaviours. Particularly, if they are not getting the mental and physical stimulation they require.

Often these dogs have either little to no outlet to fulfil their instinctive predatory drivers such as the need to herd or chase. This is why we often see working dog breeds rounding up or chasing dogs at the park, not to mention the destruction, escaping, barking and digging that goes on back at home when they have been let down by their owner.

Fortunately, there are a growing number of novice and professional dog sports on offer that can provide your working dog with an outlet to fulfil its innate desire to herd, chase, scent, retrieve and more. By getting involved you can help address some common behaviour problems, whilst providing a fun, fitness activity and helping to create greater communication and bond between dog and owner.

There are obedience and sporting clubs and competitions held all over the world for many of these activities, including:

- Obedience trials
- Agility
- Herding
- Flyball racing
- Disc Dog
- Dock jumping
- Lure coursing
- Hound trialling
- Nosework/scent detection
- Protection sports
- Earthdog trials
- Rally obedience
- Retrieving trials
- Schutzhund
- Scootering/Sled dog racing/ Bikejoring
- Canicross
- Heelwork to music
- Sighthound racing

There are many local, state and national clubs which will vary depending on where you live and the most common dog breed found in your area. So find out ways you can get involved by looking up a club close to you which suits your dog.

These sports can provide an additional outlet for your dog on a more ad hoc basis in addition to a daily enrichment plan for your dog at home. Watch them thrive at the chance to fulfil their instinctual needs through a sport tailored to their breed and abilities.

GAMES AND TRICKS TO TEACH YOUR DOG

Here's just a few games and tricks that will get both you and your dog's brain and body moving.

GAME 1 – TREAT TREASURE HUNT

Playing a treasure hunt with your dog's treats or kibble engages them mentally and physically. It taps into their natural scenting skills, which also makes them feel good. Nosework games are one of the easiest ways to tire out your dog so are a perfect game to play indoors on a rainy day.

For first timers, you may have to teach them the rules of the game (unless of course it is a very food motivated dog such as a labrador retriever, who will no doubt be over to the treat in a heartbeat).

 STEP 1

For the first couple of times, have your dog sit and wait, or restrain them on a leash, but let them watch as their treats are hidden around the room.

 STEP 2

Release your dog from their sit or leash and, when they zero in on a treat, you indicate they are correct by saying 'yes' or using a clicker (*see* p. 151), the reward then follows because they found the treat. Once they are reliably doing this, you can then add the cue 'find your treats' so you are working in some obedience training techniques too.

 STEP 3

Some dogs are quicker than others, so if your dog is a little unsure about what to do, you could gently lead or direct them over to where the treat is hidden to help.

TAP INTO THEIR NATURAL SCENTING SKILLS

🐾 STEP 4

After you are confident that your dog understands what 'find your treats' means, you can start making it a bit more challenging – have them stay in another room when you hide the treats.

🐾 STEP 5

As they get better at the game, you can then start to hide the treats in places that really require them to use their nose, such as under a rug or even in an object like a paper cup.

The great thing about this game is that you can use it as you are leaving your dog alone for a while to reduce both boredom and anxiety, particularly once they have a strong association with 'find your treats'. Simply hide some treats around the house or yard and, as you leave, give them the cue phrase 'find your treats' so they have a positive association with your departure as they go off hunting for food.

GAME 2 – HUMAN HIDE-AND-SEEK

As you might guess, this is pretty much the same as what we played as children. It can be played indoors, in the yard and even when you are out on a walk (as long as you have a good recall and don't have a dog that has anxiety and is likely to panic when they can't see you). My mum loves playing this with her dog Joe and uses it to help improve his recall.

🐾 STEP 1

Wait until your dog is distracted and quickly find a hiding place like a tree or bush. Don't go too far if you are out in public so that you can still keep an eye on your dog, and quickly step out and get their attention if they start to panic. If you are indoors, wait until your dog is in another room then go hide somewhere.

🐾 STEP 2

Call out to them in a really excitable loud voice. My mum does a long shrill 'Jooooooooooeeeee!' call which he now knows means 'game on!'. You might need to call out a few times if they can't quite pick up the direction of your sound.

🐾 STEP 3

Give them lots of praise and pats when they find you. Remember, make it fun!

The more you play it the better they will get at finding you quickly, so make sure you change the types of places you hide behind or in.

GAME 3 – TIDY UP YOUR TOYS

There are a few ways to teach this trick, so I'm going with the easiest one. If your dog gets very excited and distracted by toys (again, yes I'm talking about you, Darcy!) then try it after a walk. You'll need to make sure your dog is reliably offering the first step before moving onto the second step and so on, so it isn't going to be mastered in a day, maybe not even a month. Take it slowly and be consistent.

🐾 STEP 1 – FIND A HOME FOR YOUR DOG'S TOY BOX

While you are teaching your dog this trick, you'll need to make sure you leave the toy box in the same spot while the training continues. Moving it will confuse your dog.

🐾 STEP 2 – PICK HIS FAVOURITE TOY

Call or walk your dog over to the basket and give him his favourite toy so he has it in his mouth.

🐾 STEP 3 – GET HIS ATTENTION INSIDE THE TOY BOX

To bring his attention inside the toy box, point or click your fingers in it so that his head is over the inside of the toy box, still holding the toy.

🐾 STEP 4 – ADD THE 'CUE'

Offer your dog a high value treat reward (soft, smelly and squishy treats work best in training ... or roast chicken as the ultimate reward) and say 'tidy up' as he drops the toy into the basket to take the treat. Again, I always like to mark this desired behaviour with a 'yes' or a clicker for consistency in training, so do that as soon as it drops, and give him the treat and add some praise too, if you like, when he drops the toy.

🐾 STEP 5 – PRACTISE, PRACTISE, PRACTISE

The key to training games like this is to keep it short and fun, so repeat this process with your dog five times in a row, several times a day for a few weeks, until he starts to show he is really understanding what to do and reliably drops the toy when you say 'tidy up', then start to move farther away from the toy box.

Not too far or fast, remember we slowly increase the distance and distraction. When you say the command, he should know to drop the toy in the basket and make sure you give him lots of praise.

GAME 4 – THE 'HIGH FIVE'

A neat little trick to teach your dog and impress your mates when your football team scores a goal, is teaching your dog to 'high five' you. It's a nice simple one too.

🐾 STEP 1

Have your dog sit and hold a treat in front of him.

🐾 STEP 2

Wait patiently as he starts smelling or licking or nudging your hand, keeping your hand firmly closed and staying still.

🐾 STEP 3

Your dog will eventually start using his paw to tap your hand and immediately as he does this, say 'yes' and release the treat.

🐾 STEP 4

Keep repeating this a few times until he is reliably going straight to use his paw and as he starts to move it towards you add the cue word, 'high five'.

🐾 STEP 5

Once this is consistently happening, start presenting your open hand in the high five position. You may need to hide a small piece of treat between your fingers to entice him. Keep it there until he touches it with his paw and keep saying 'high five' with the action. As soon as he touches your hand with his paw, again reward him with the treat and praise.

🐾 STEP 6

Gradually phase out the treats by rewarding him instead with praise. As he starts to perform the action reliably on cue, you can then reward him with a treat for a particularly good and fast response. Again, this surprise bonus of a treat (or whatever is considered the highest reward) from time to time encourages your dog to continue improving their response. A bit like how the lure of a cash bonus for human employees at the end of the year for a job well done can provide added incentive.

GAME 5 – PLAY DEAD

🐾 STEP 1 – START IN A DROP/DOWN POSITION

To teach your dog this game you will need to have your dog trained to do the drop/down position and have them comfortable and reliable at doing this.

🐾 STEP 2 – USE A TREAT TO ROLL YOUR DOG OVER

Hold a treat close to your dog's nose, and slowly move it up and over to your dog's side so they are following you with their nose close to the treat, to the point their body has to follow and roll over onto the side to get the treat.

🐾 STEP 3 – MARK AND REWARD

As soon as your dog is lying on its side, use your 'yes' or clicker to quickly indicate that is the position you want and then give your dog his treat. Repeat these steps several times until your dog is comfortably and reliably rolling over to get the treat. Practise this initial step in short, two- or three-minute sessions a few times a day.

🐾 STEP 4 – ADD THE VERBAL CUE

After your dog is reliably completing this action and doing well at laying on his side, add a verbal cue word such as 'bang' or 'dead'. (You can work on holding them in their position too by slowly extending out the time between the 'yes' and giving them the treat that signals their release.)

🐾 STEP 5 – ADD THE VISUAL CUE

When your dog gets the hang of the verbal cue, add a **visual cue** such as making a shooting signal with your right index finger and thumb, and quickly say your cue word.

🐾 STEP 6 – PRACTISE A FEW TIMES A DAY FOR A FEW MINUTES AT A TIME

Practise this trick several times a day for a few minutes each time, until your dog is reliably falling to its side in response to the signal.

Withhold the treat for longer periods of time after you have marked the roll over with the 'yes' or clicker if you want to extend out how long you want them to play dead for. Remember not to move ahead too quickly. You may need to go back a few steps if your dog is having trouble; patience is the key.

LOVE

BUILDING A BOND

My morning routine starts with Darcy poking his little head out from his sleeping bag to see if I'm awake. Usually I am, as it is my movement that entices him out of his warm comfy den as he waits for me to turn and smile at him which is his cue to come completely out to get his morning ear massage or tummy rub.

It is those little moments and interactions that you share with your dog which really facilitate and strengthen your bond.

Feeding, walking, playing, training and grooming are all very important aspects of caring for your dog, but loving words, snuggling up on the couch and giving them a gentle massage or tummy rub each day allows you to really get to know your dog's personality and little quirks. This not only helps soothe and relax them, but you'll also reap the benefits of taking some time out of your day to simply be in the moment with your dog, because, let's face it, dogs have got living in the present totally worked out.

Spending time each day sharing loving moments and providing an environment of mutual love and respect for your dog also promotes trust in your dog. This can go a long way in helping a fearful dog build up their confidence, which in turn can help

IS IT EAR RUB TIME?

address some fear-based behaviour issues. The stronger your bond, the more your dog pays attention and listens to you, which further helps with obedience and training.

Owning a dog requires commitment and love

Sadly, far too many people decide to get a dog for all of the wrong reasons, without knowing or being prepared to put in the time and effort required to provide a dog with the love, guidance and care it deserves.

A 2018 UK study found that undesirable behaviours are a substantial risk factor for dogs under the age of three years, with behavioural issues such as aggression, anxiety, destructive and disobedient behaviour being the major reason for surrendered dogs being euthanised.

What happens to a puppy in their first four months of life is critical to forming its behaviour and memories, good and bad. I believe that undesirable behaviours are often the direct result of the dog being let down by the humans during this important period. I have seen first-hand how pounds and shelters are full of young dogs who have been surrendered through no fault of their own – they have not been given the proper care or socialisation during this critical period of development.

It breaks my heart to see these innocent faces looking so distraught and confused as they are left all alone in a strange and scary environment. This is why it is my mission to help change this through better education and increased awareness about what it takes to own and properly take care of a dog for its *entire* life.

BEFORE YOU GET A DOG

Do your homework

Whether you are getting a new puppy or adopting a rescue dog, you need to do your homework:

- Research the common traits/temperament of the breed you are thinking about

- What are their common health issues and dietary considerations?

- Do they have specific exercise needs – mental and physical?

- If you are looking to rescue, ask about and ensure you understand any behaviour issues a particular dog may have. Are you equipped and prepared to put in the time and money that may be required for training and veterinary care, particularly for any fear and anxiety, aggression, phobias or health issues they may have?

As always, it's important to remember that while a breed may have a general personality and disposition, every dog is still an individual that requires good training and the right level of attention, exercise and care to keep them and your family happy and safe. Not all dogs suit all lifestyles and if we don't get it right it can cause issues for both the human and our furry family members.

Things to consider

FAMILY SITUATION

- Do you have young kids or are you planning to have children in the future?

- If so, is the breed, size and temperament suitable for babies, toddlers, children?

- Will a dog get the attention/exercise they need once kids come along? Behaviour issues can often develop when a dog is relegated to the backyard once a new baby arrives, which can lead to resentment and a negative association with the baby

- Are you able and prepared to do the work required to ensure a smooth introduction, and continue showing your dog the love and positive reinforcement it requires to ensure harmony in a household with dogs and children?

LIFESTYLE

- Will everyone in your household be out at work all day leaving them home alone?

- Do you have an active or sedentary lifestyle? How would this impact on your dog's need for daily exercise? Would they join you on your sporting endeavours and is this appropriate for the breed, age etc.?

- Do you go away on holidays or are you out a lot? If the answer is yes, are you prepared to take them with you?

HOME ENVIRONMENT

🐾 How much room/exercise does the breed need and does your home environment cater for this?

🐾 Do you have a backyard or live in an apartment and is this suitable for the dog/breed you are considering?

🐾 Does it provide adequate shelter and safety?

🐾 Do you rent – what if you move? You might be in a place that accepts pets now, but what are your options if you have to move and can't take them with you? Do you have family that they are happy with that can help or would you have to surrender them?

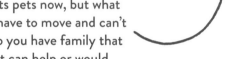

TENS OF THOUSANDS OF PETS ARE SURRENDERED IN AUSTRALIA ALONE AS A RESULT OF PEOPLE HAVING TO MOVE INTO RENTAL ACCOMMODATION

FINANCES

The average life of a dog is 10 years, but many small or medium dogs live much longer, costing on average A$25,000 over their lifetime in Australia. In the UK, reports put it at between £21,000 and £33,000 depending on size and breed, and almost USD$16,000 on average in America.

🐾 Can you afford to provide your dog, particularly a large breed or multiple dogs, with the quality diet required to help ensure they have the best chance of good health and behaviour?

🐾 Dogs need monthly flea/worm/other treatments, annual vaccinations, regular grooming and other health care so are you able to afford to provide these now, and what position would you be in should your work or family circumstances change and impact on your financial circumstances?

🐾 Can you afford the money and time to do dog training and socialisation with a puppy, older or rescue dog?

EMOTIONAL TIME AND EFFORT

🐾 Are you prepared to do the training and socialisation dogs need as a puppy, as well as the ongoing training for adult dogs to help curb any behaviour issues?

🐾 Will you provide them with the daily environmental enrichment they need for their age and breed?

🐾 Are you able/willing to provide your dog with the level of human interaction dogs need and invest the time to create a bond that helps to develop mutual trust and respect?

Dogs need human company, daily play, training and socialisation, human company and interactions, and much more to keep them mentally and physically stimulated. Does your lifestyle really suit having a dog right now and in the long term?

FINDING A FURRY FRIEND

Adopting a rescue dog

Although many dogs end up in a pound or animal shelter due to behavioural issues, getting a dog from a pound or shelter does not mean you will be landed with a damaged or badly-behaved dog. Many of these so-called undesirable behaviours, even aggressive behaviour, are usually because the dog has not received the care and direction it needs, causing anxiety or boredom and these can be overcome with the love and commitment of a new family.

By bringing a rescue dog into your family you still have to do all of this training, socialisation and a raft of environmental enrichment activities and care. You may have to enlist the help of a professional trainer to assist you with some of the tougher problems, but you generally don't have to go through the sleepless nights and toilet training required with getting a new puppy. A good shelter or rescue group will also be able to provide you with background on the dog, their personality, quirks, habits and training needs so you can be prepared.

WHY IS IT SO HARD TO ADOPT A DOG SOMETIMES?

Don't be surprised if the rescue group does a rigorous check on you and your family situation. It is important to remember that some of their dogs have already had a very rough start in life and may have been in the shelter system for a while through no fault of their own, so it is for the safety and wellbeing of all parties involved that this level of assessment is required.

NEVER JUDGE A BOOK BY ITS COVER

The biggest mistake people make is looking at the dog breed label on a shelter kennel. My Mum always told me to never judge a book by its cover, which is perhaps why I am so passionate about <u>not</u> putting labels on a dog based on its breed. From my own personal experience, the dogs that dish out the most bites and react with fear or aggression to other dogs and people are not the so-called dangerous breeds that the media and general public are quick to judge and destroy.

Sometimes the breed label is removed in a shelter and dogs are selected by their new owners purely based on their behaviour and interactions with people and even what people *believe* the breed to be when it is, in fact, totally different. In most instances the true breed of a dog that ends up in a pound or shelter is unknown, so their breed label is often a guess based on what they look like. Sadly however, people tend to make assumptions about a dog's personality and future behaviour based on these guesses and can find themselves making the wrong choice as a result.

GET TO KNOW THE DOG AND ITS BACKGROUND

When adopting a dog, it is important that you take the time to get to know the dog you are interested in. Don't go for one based on look or breed, but rather spend time interacting with them and make sure you read the PLAY section of this book, if you haven't already, to familiarise yourself with the signs to look out for in a dog's body language (*see* pp. 117–122) to get a feel for how they are really feeling and what they are saying to you.

Ask the shelter or rescue group for a full behaviour assessment. Most will be honest with you about any issues that need addressing, so you need to ask as many questions as you can and spend as much time with them as possible. But be aware some shelters are understaffed, under-resourced and under pressure to make room for more dogs so they may

TAKE THE TIME TO GET TO KNOW THE DOG YOU LIKE

be focussed on finding a new home for a dog as quickly as possible. It is up to you to ask lots of questions and be honest about what your capabilities are.

BECOME A FOSTER CARER FIRST

You can provide short-term or emergency care which can help save and improve a dog's life. Some shelters have even introduced one and two-night sleepovers which have been proven to help reduce the stress hormone levels in shelter dogs and help them to be more rested during and immediately following a sleepover. Contact your local shelter to see if they offer foster arrangements.

BENEFITS OF BECOMING A FOSTER CARER

- Allows you to assess if you are ready for a dog without the long-term commitment
- Companionship for current dog and allows you to see how they respond to a new dog in the family
- Frees up room at shelter to save another life
- Helps train/overcome their fear of humans and other dogs – better chance of rehoming
- Access a support network from the rescue group and other volunteers
- Helps put you in the front of the queue to adopting a dog
- You may become a foster fail ... meaning you have found your pawfect match!

SO, YOU WANT A PUPPY?

There are various avenues for finding a puppy, some are okay and others are not. If you are determined to buy a pedigree puppy, the best place to start is to contact the breeders' association for the breed you are interested in. Or if a friend has the breed of dog you are after and it has a good temperament and health, that is a great place to start too.

Puppies are also available in pet stores or online or via social media, I do not recommend this. While some reputable breeders do advertise their puppies online, purchasing a puppy online is opening yourself up to the potential of being scammed, supporting puppy mills or unethical breeders.

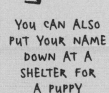

YOU CAN ALSO
PUT YOUR NAME
DOWN AT A
SHELTER FOR
A PUPPY

How to avoid backyard breeders

- 🐾 Never pay for a dog or a puppy you have only seen online before you pick him up

- 🐾 If buying from a pet store, ask where they get their puppies from and ask for evidence? How can you really know?

- 🐾 Don't believe what a website or Facebook page says, even if the breeder looks good with happy pictures and testimonials – these can be fake

- 🐾 Ask around – people you trust or those with a well behaved and healthy breed you are also wanting at the local dog park or obedience schools

DO YOUR RESEARCH!

- 🐾 Is it really where they live? Visit the home, no halfway meeting point or car drop off

- 🐾 Talk to local pounds, shelters and rescue groups as they often see a pattern of dogs coming in and out or being surrendered and can identify from where

- 🐾 Talk to your local council or government office's animal welfare officers

- 🐾 If it sounds too good, is too cheap or too easy to be true, then it is

Assess parental traits and health

- Ask to meet the puppy's mother. If the breeder says no, you need to question why not

- Watch the mother's interactions, is she ignoring them or aggressive to you or the puppies?

- How do the puppies interact, are they confident, biting, cowering, inquisitive?

- How many litters has she had?

- What is the environment like, does she appear stressed or anxious (*see* pp. 117–122 on how to read the signs)?

- Ask for health tests that are relevant for the particular breed, particularly for health conditions they may be predisposed to

- Ask for their vet clinic and visit to discuss

Get to know the puppies

- What early socialisation have they had with other people?

- You need to think carefully, rather than just taking the one that looks pretty

- Take the time to get to know the puppies, ask questions, don't believe everything you are told

- If they are the last one in the litter, the 'special one', question why … usually there is a reason they are the last to go

When you find the right one

- Take a blanket or piece of clothing to leave with the mother and puppies, to bring back home with you when you pick up your puppy as it will provide a comforting smell of the mother

- Find out what they are being fed, refer to EAT (*see* pp. 1–95) to choose the best diet that you can provide, don't just take the breeder's advice

WHAT YOU'LL NEED FOR YOUR NEW PUPPY OR DOG

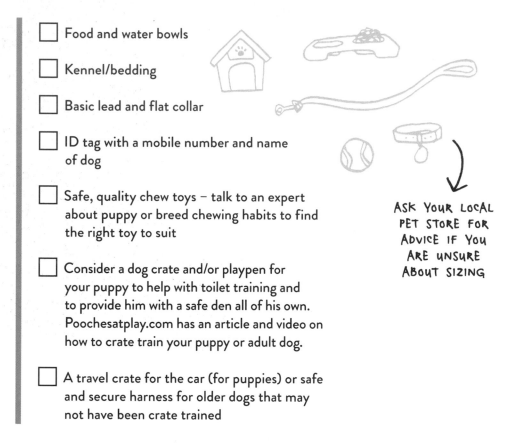

- [ ] Food and water bowls

- [ ] Kennel/bedding

- [ ] Basic lead and flat collar

- [ ] ID tag with a mobile number and name of dog

- [ ] Safe, quality chew toys – talk to an expert about puppy or breed chewing habits to find the right toy to suit

- [ ] Consider a dog crate and/or playpen for your puppy to help with toilet training and to provide him with a safe den all of his own. Poochesatplay.com has an article and video on how to crate train your puppy or adult dog.

- [ ] A travel crate for the car (for puppies) or safe and secure harness for older dogs that may not have been crate trained

ASK YOUR LOCAL PET STORE FOR ADVICE IF YOU ARE UNSURE ABOUT SIZING

Microchips and ID tags

If your dog goes missing, one of the ways to increase the chances of finding him is having him microchipped. Talk to your vet to find out the most common microchip used in your area as not all scanners pick up all microchips in some countries. It is vital if you change phone numbers or move home that you update your contact details, so do ask your vet to regularly scan the chip to ensure its readable and hasn't moved around.

All European Union (EU) member countries, Australia and many other countries require that a pet microchip be implanted in your dog to identify it. No state in the US imposes mandatory microchipping, although there are some municipalities which have such laws. Sadly, up to 8 million animals end up in shelters every year but only 15%-20% of dogs and less than 2% of cats are ever reclaimed by their owners and they are either rehomed or euthanised due to contact details not being up-to-date.

Your pet should also have a collar with tags on it. With cats you want to use breakaway collars so they don't get caught when they're climbing. You can't just assume the person who finds your pet will know anything about microchips. But if your phone number is right there, everyone knows what to do with that.

TAKING YOUR NEW DOG HOME

Planning the day of pick-up is really important so that you can help make this experience is as calm and stress free for you and your puppy or rescue dog as possible.

If you are driving a long distance home, dogs can get motion sickness, like us humans do, so again refer to poochesatplay.com for my articles and videos on how to deal with this and anxiety associated with car travel.

- Make sure you stop regularly for toilet breaks and a drink of water

- Ensure they have plenty of fresh air from an open window or circulating air

- If you are taking the kids along make sure they keep calm so as not to stress out the new puppy

- Take along some small, healthy treats and the blanket you left with his mother and siblings to provide some comfort

IT'S A GOOD IDEA TO PACK THESE ITEMS TO BE WELL-PREPARED FOR THE JOURNEY

- correct sized collar and lead to keep them secure on stops
- blanket or towel
- water and bowl
- poop bags
- antibacterial hand gel
- cleaning wipes

Remember to praise and reward your new puppy for calm behaviour, and be careful not to reinforce anxious behaviour like shaking, whining, barking etc. You can provide them comfort *see* p. 202 where I talk about how to be careful not to reinforce anxiety in your dog.

ARRIVING HOME

- Give your puppy space and time to sniff around and check out its new surroundings

- If you have another dog:

  - Introduce them slowly – let them sniff and interact with each other at their own pace

  - Ideally start off the introduction with an on-lead walk

  - Don't leave them alone unsupervised early on

  - Put away any items your current dog may be inclined to resource guard over such as toys or food

  - Create a positive association with the new dog by rewarding your current dog for friendly, calm and welcoming behaviour

  - Do not punish either dog if they show signs of being unhappy or fearful, *see* pp. 117–122 to read about body language and tips on dealing with dog to dog reactivity

- New dogs and cats should be kept apart in separate rooms for a few days at least to start with so they can smell each other through the doors but are not forced to be with one another. Check out my video on introducing cats and dogs on poochesatplay.com

ENSURE YOUR HOME IS SAFE AND SECURE

- Look for escape routes. If your puppy can fit its head through a gap or hole in a fence, then it is likely to be able to get its body through

- Make sure all gates and fences, especially pool gates, are secure

- Check access to under the house or behind sheds so they can't get stuck

- If you live in an apartment and have a balcony, or if your rescue dog or puppy is a breed that can easily scale fences as it grows, make sure any gaps are closed off, and that there is nothing puppy can climb up on ... and over! Lattice slanted inwards can be applied to the top of fencing to deter a crafty escape artist

- Check for any exposed wiring, toys, clothing and other things puppies or anxious dogs are likely to chew

- Store any chemicals or garden products safely away

- Make sure you research any potential toxic plants you may have in your garden as again, puppies love to chew

SET CLEAR BOUNDARIES FOR YOUR DOG ... AND STICK TO THEM!

Start training immediately and set clear boundaries:

- Where they can and can't go in the house

- What they can and can't sit or jump up on such as the couch or bed

- What is and isn't acceptable behaviour in general

Some common mistakes families make include:

- Some members of the family letting or encouraging a dog to sit or sleep on the couch or bed when others aren't there

- Someone feeding them scraps under the table

- Patting them when they jump up on people or bark for attention when you actually want them to act calmly or sit to wait to be called over

Everyone in the family needs to reward and therefore reinforce the desired behaviour you want at the time your dog is doing it. They also need to ignore or not encourage unwanted behaviour, even inadvertently. For more about being a good firm but fair leader, avoiding reinforcing any anxiety and spending time training and building your bond see pp. 166–167.

GETTING A SECOND DOG FOR COMPANY

IS IT REALLY A GOOD IDEA?

I often hear people say they want to get a second dog as company for their current dog because it suffers from anxiety, barks all day, keeps trying to escape and so on, thinking getting another dog will solve all of their problems. The reality is that you may actually make the problem worse and you could end up with two barkers, escape artists and generally double trouble on your hands.

Many anxious or bored dogs who display this kind of behaviour due to a lack of mental and physical stimulation can trigger the other dog to follow their lead. Two dogs left alone in a backyard all day aren't necessarily going to think 'great, let's play shall we' and could dislike each other, so you may end up with two fighting, anxious and bored dogs on your hands as well.

However, if your dog loves the company of other dogs and is eager to play as much as possible with a fellow furry friend, they may welcome a new addition with a wagging tail and propensity for fun into the home. An older dog may also get a fresh lease on life with a younger buddy for company, but don't take anything for granted and assume this will be the case. This is another reason why spending time getting to know your dog and understanding their likes and dislikes, quirks and idiosyncrasies is so important.

If you still want to get another dog but are unsure, chat to your vet, trial your dog in doggy daycare or group walking with a dog trainer so you can get a professional opinion. You should try to address any behaviour issues your current dog is displaying before you take the plunge. Again, this is another reason why becoming a foster carer can be a valuable exercise.

I often watch Darcy and the other dogs that come stay at our place with a bit of a smirk as they take turns claiming each other's bed, sneaking off with a toy, refusing to give up in a game of tug-of-war and sneaking in to swap meals because the other one looks like it might have something more appealing on offer (generally they are the same!).

If tempers do start to rise due to the threat of losing out on a valuable resource or adrenaline starts to surge during a tussle over a toy, generally a firm 'hey, stop it' is enough to bring them back to their senses. In Darcy's case, who can be inclined to try to resource guard over me or a toy every now and then and gets a warning, he'll leave the toy and allow his buddy to pick it up and take it away (reluctantly, I might add). If he can get away with it though he might quietly grab it when no one is looking and go and hide it in the corners of his bed!

In multiple dog households where this starts to become a bit more common and the fighting starts to become both more frequent and increases in intensity, it is usually because stress and anxiety levels have begun to rise over time and you need to get to the bottom of what's going on.

HOW TO MANAGE A MULTIPLE-DOG HOUSEHOLD

🐾 If the tussles between the two dogs are nothing more than some spats here and there, and neither dog seems to be showing ongoing signs of stress or anxiety, then you can often mitigate against the problem by controlling the resources

🐾 If your dogs tend to fight over food, then feed them separately

🐾 Teach them place training such as 'on your bed' and teach them to play with their own toys when they are in their own place (and not to sneak off over to the other's place and steal their toy) ... yes, Darcy, that is directed at you!

🐾 Don't force them to be friends or play together when they want their space. If they can be in the same room together minding their own business, then let them live in harmony without forcing the issue of friendship

🐾 Share the love, pats and praise and put it on your terms i.e. don't let one demand all of your attention or but in when you are patting the other

🐾 To help with this, work on your obedience training with each of them separately so that you can ask one to sit or go to their place, whilst you call the other over, then do the same to the other

🐾 Set clear boundaries and restrict access to areas if they resource guard over rooms, chairs, beds etc. Ensure all family members do the same!

🐾 Reward calm, friendly co-operative behaviour so that it is reinforced

🐾 Avoid or remove them from any known trigger situations

If the fighting between your dogs has become serious and there is intent or accidental injury, then it is time to seek out the services of a professional vet behaviourist or dog trainer. In some cases, dogs may have to live separately in the house. Kept to different rooms at all times, walked or let inside or outside at different times. This might sound harsh, but it is an alternative to rehoming one of the dogs if the situation becomes dangerous. I have seen this be successfully implemented with a client and it has allowed both dogs to remain with their family, keeping the older one that was being regularly attacked safe, and reducing the stress levels of both dogs and everyone else in the household too.

It is important that you also have all dogs checked over by a vet if the behaviour is out of character, to pick up any medical issues or pain. It may not always be the older or sick dog acting out either, the healthy one could be picking up on the illness in the other dog. Changes in home environment and routine can also be a cause.

TAKING CARE OF YOUR DOG'S HEALTH

Providing your dog with the love and care they need includes protecting him from some of the most common and not so common threats to their health and wellbeing. This includes ensuring they are protected from life-threatening canine diseases, physical ailments and everyday risks and upsets.

Don't miss your annual vet visit

Unfortunately, our four-legged friends age much faster than we do, with one human year being roughly equivalent to seven dog years. This is why an annual visit to the vet is so important.

Having a full examination of your dog every year can help uncover any sources of pain or ill health that you may not have picked up on or that your dog may be hiding (which dogs do!). It also means that you can discuss your flea, tick and worming treatments, check their weight and discuss any dietary concerns or changes to their diet that may be needed as they age, have an annual professional dental clean and discuss any other concerns you may have.

Vaccinations

Most animals need core vaccines that protect them from severe, life-threatening diseases for their species that have global distribution.

Three core vaccines for dogs are those recommended by the World Small Animal Veterinary Association and are referred to as the C3 vaccinations:

- Canine distemper

- Hepatitis (Adenovirus)

- Parvovirus

Additional vaccines which may be required for kennel boarding, dog daycare, travel and even grooming are:

- Parainfluenza (kennel cough)

- Bordetella (canine cough)

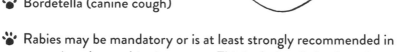

CHECK WITH YOUR VET WHAT IS REQUIRED IN YOUR COUNTRY

- Rabies may be mandatory or is at least strongly recommended in countries where rabies is present. This includes all the Americas, Asia, Africa, the Middle East and some parts of Europe.

Newborn puppies receive their initial C3 vaccines in their first 6–8 weeks of life when they have some protection through antibodies from their vaccinated mother's milk. Additional boosters are administered at intervals up until 4 months when their immune systems are functional and protective.

The Australian Veterinary Association recommends that the core vaccines be given to all adult animals every 3 years. This is based on recent scientific research which shows that effectiveness of many vaccines may be substantially longer than 12 months. The only exception is the first adult vaccine – this should be given after 12 months.

Titer testing, which is a simple blood test, is now available to assist pet parents that are concerned about over-vaccination and want to know if their dog still has the antibodies to a particular virus or bacteria before deciding on whether they need a booster or not. You will need to check however if a Titer Test is considered acceptable vaccination documentation for kennel boarding etc. in your region, as it is not in all circumstances.

Allergies

The signs of an allergy in your dog are similar to those we get and include excessive itching and scratching, rashes, sneezing, watery eyes and skin inflammation.

When it comes to allergies and pets, many dog owners believe their dog's food is the culprit, see p. 19 for more information. However, flea allergies have been on the rise over the past 10 years with a 12% increase in dogs and a whopping 67% increase in cats!

YOUR VET CAN HELP

Environmental allergies are also on an upward trend, with a more than 30% increase in dogs and 11% increase in cats over this time. Although environmental allergens for pets will vary by region and climate, some of the common causes are the same as they are for us humans including pollen, moulds, animal dander (the stuff that sheds from their skin), cleaning solutions and medication.

Fleas

If you see your dog scratching more than usual, I find the best way to
check if fleas are the culprit is to part their hair above their rump so
you can see their skin and see if you can find flea dirt, which is black
flea droppings. Also check the exposed skin on the inside of their legs
and belly as you often find a little critter crawling around once you start
running your fingers around their hiding places.

The flea cycle is a vicious one and requires you to do more than just get
rid of them off your dog. You have to treat them AND the environment as
well. **Prevention** is better than cure!

Here are my tips to keep your dog and home flea free:

Repellents – Repellents are the cornerstone of prevention and can
include natural repellent sprays and washes, topical insecticides or

tablets. Some kill fleas and ticks as well as other parasites such as worms, so check the label carefully. Talk to your vet or pet store staff member to ensure you are choosing the right one for your dog's size and region you live in or may be visiting.

Routine checking – Look for fleas, ticks and coat abnormalities any time you brush or shampoo your dog or cat, or when you return home from areas that are likely to have higher numbers of these parasites.

Wash bedding in hot water – Wash your dog's bed and bedding in hot water at minimum 60°C (140F) at least every couple of weeks. You will also need to wash your own bedding or any other blankets or washable items the dog may sleep on or have access to if you find a flea on him.

Vacuum – You'll also need to vacuum the floors and furniture that your pet comes in contact with. Careful and regular vacuuming/cleaning of the pet's living area helps to remove and kill flea eggs, and larvae.

Home insecticides – You may also have to treat your house with insecticides if the problem keeps occurring. Never leave your pets inside during use and read the instructions to find out how long before you and your pets can go back inside.

Shampoos – Flea and tick shampoos help to rid your pet of the fleas and ticks he already has. There are some shampoos that use natural pyrethrin to kill the fleas rather than chemicals.

Flea/lice combs – Flea/lice combs are a safe method to use on ill, pregnant or young pets. Place the fleas you comb off in water with detergent added to kill them.

By the way I just have to ask this question ... who started itching when I started talking about fleas? ☺ I did!

Ticks

CHECK US FOR TICKS PLEASE!

Unlike fleas, flies and lice, which are insects, ticks are arachnids that attach themselves to animals and people, feed on blood and transmit diseases directly into their host's system. They are capable of spreading serious infectious diseases (such as Lyme disease, Rocky Mountain Spotted Fever and others) to pets and people.

REMEMBER
As with flea prevention, tick repellent in the form of topical applications, tablets and sprays is also vital where your dog may be at risk.

HOW DO I KNOW IF MY PET HAS A TICK?
It is a good idea to check your dog for ticks after they have been out on walks, especially if they have been into the countryside and walked through long grass, and particularly if you live in areas known for ticks.

You will find them around your dog's neck, in the ears, in the folds between the legs and the body, and between the toes. Ticks come in different sizes. Some are tiny, but visible to the naked eye. However, they can be hidden under his fur so the best way to check for ticks is by carefully feeling your dog's body.

You might also notice your dog licking excessively in the spot where the tick is.

WHAT TO DO IF YOU FIND A TICK
Ticks need to be carefully removed. Use caution because contact with the tick's blood is what transmits infection. First, treat the affected area with rubbing alcohol. Then, gently pluck the tick from your dog's body

with tweezers. Make sure you remove all of the tick's body, including its biting head.

Some ticks can cause paralysis and other life-threatening illnesses so you should always have your dog evaluated by your veterinarian as soon as possible after you find ticks on him because you can't be sure that you've removed all of the tick or that it hasn't already transmitted disease. Your vet can perform appropriate blood tests to identify or rule out disease.

How worms can affect your dog and you

Worms have a serious health effect on dogs and cats, so intestinal worming should never be overlooked. Particularly as they can also be passed on to humans.

You can actually see tapeworms and roundworms. Tapeworms look like small pieces of rice and can be found in the faeces or around the tail and rear area of your dog. This is why you might see your dog scoot his rear across the ground. Roundworms are long white worms that look like spaghetti. You might notice them in a puppy's vomit or also seen in faeces. (I really hope you weren't eating as you started to read this).

Regularly worming your pet is one of the easiest ways to make sure they (and you!) stay worm free, so talk to your vet or pet store staff member to find the right worming treatment for your pet. It is also important to pick up your pet's droppings and to wash hands after playing with pets and before eating.

HEARTWORM – PREVENTION VERSUS CURE

In the case of heartworm, prevention is the option you should always choose because the treatment for it is not only costly and difficult, but the treatment itself can even cause death.

Some dogs may even require surgery to remove all of the worms from their heart chambers after treatment, so when you consider how easy it is to access heartworm treatment and the low cost of it, there is no reason to not have your dog's heartworm up-to-date all year round.

Unfortunately, there are still many people who are unaware of how dangerous the heartworm can be, so please don't be one of those owners who leaves it to chance.

Oral care

Over 80% of dogs over the age of three have active dental disease which can cause pain for your dog. Dogs instinctively hide signs of periodontitis (gum disease) and often by the time signs are visible, the damage has already been done and your dog is suffering.

According to the World Small Animal Veterinary Association (WSAVA) there is evidence that periodontal disease is linked to heart disease and diabetes, while it can also impact on liver and kidney disease, as well as jaw fractures due to bone destruction around the teeth.

SYMPTOMS OF GUM DISEASE:

- Bleeding or red gums
- Blood on toys
- Bad breath
- Loose teeth

- Head shyness and excessive salivation
- Chewing on one side or problems picking up food
- Sneezing or nasal discharge

To help assess the health of your dog's teeth and to identify any gum disease or other issues, you really do need to see your veterinarian, which again is why the annual visit is so important. When it comes to treatment, a dental scale and polish under general anaesthetic is done, and any loose teeth or those with painful decay may need to be removed.

TIPS FOR PREVENTING DENTAL DISEASE

- Daily brushing! You will need a dog toothbrush, baby toothbrush or finger brush and dog specific toothpaste as well. Ask your local veterinary clinic to demonstrate the technique

- Start slowly, one tooth at a time and reward your dog with praise when they allow you to clean the tooth so that they have a good association with the process. Build up to more teeth with positive reinforcement

- Annual dental examination by a qualified veterinarian, which may also result in a scale and clean under anaesthetic if signs of plaque or gum disease are evident

- Chew toys, all natural dental sticks or raw meaty bones may also assist (*see* pp. 70–71 on feeding bones), but these are not enough on their own

- Dental-specific water additives can also assist, as *may* dental specific kibble if a complete dental program is also implemented

Canine cancer

Common symptoms that may indicate canine cancer include: rapid weight loss, reduction in appetite, unwillingness to exercise, visible lumps or growths on the skin, difficulty swallowing, breathing or going to the toilet, coughing, vomiting or lameness. However, these symptoms are common to a large number of illnesses, so a thorough check up by your vet will be required to determine the cause, with cancer sometimes being the remaining diagnosis when all other possible causes have been ruled out.

Your dog's cancer treatment will be determined by your veterinarian or veterinary oncologist and will depend on the type of cancer, as well as other factors specific to your dog. Your vet may recommend chemotherapy, radiation, surgery, or a combination of these treatments. It's important to note that when treating dogs, the goal of cancer treatment is entering remission, not curing it. Our dogs do live shorter lives than us and as dogs can't understand what is going on, we do not want them to feel sick during treatment so they are given lower doses.

Bones and joints

As many as 1 in 5 dogs will have a joint issue or mobility problem. Some of the common joint injuries that dogs experience, and which can cause chronic pain and a reduction in quality of life if left untreated, can come about due to injuries, old age or genetics. The most common injuries are cruciate injury, elbow dysplasia, slipped discs in back and hip dysplasia. Most of these ailments occur without warning and costly treatment is often required quite rapidly to ensure your dog has the best possible prognosis.

Some mild signs can be expected as pets age such as a reluctance to use stairs or not jumping as readily as they once may have or even tiring more readily when walking. However, there could be more significant underlying health issues that create these symptoms, so it is important to consult a veterinarian as soon as you notice these signs. A diet rich in Omega-3 fatty acids, glucosamine and chondroitin may also help, particularly as dogs age.

PET INSURANCE

Seeing a vet can be expensive so getting pet insurance for your dog from when they are a puppy can provide you with peace of mind and the protection you may need as they go through their life stages. We all know that accidents can happen at any time; puppies in particular seem to regularly ingest a wide variety of objects, so your pet insurance cover may pay for itself in those first couple of years of your dog's life, when they are at their most inquisitive and still learning. But like any insurance, make sure you check the fine print for details that may exclude or restrict coverage for your dog.

Some of the other benefits of pet insurance I believe is to help ensure that should your dog have an accident or a life-threatening injury, you are not faced with the heart-breaking decision of having to euthanise your best buddy simply because you can't afford the costly surgery. Many people also say they will save the money each week instead; I find this rarely actually happens.

TOP TIPS TO HELP AN ANXIOUS DOG

Avoid reinforcing the fear

During a stressful moment it is important to keep calm yourself and act as normally as possible. No yelling at your dog to be quiet or to toughen up, but, likewise, no baby voices, hugging or picking them up, all of which can reinforce or encourage their fears.

Teach your dog 'look at me' (*see* p. 113) so you can distract him from reacting to a trigger. In instances where your dog does not react to the trigger and remains calm, it is important you reward this desired behaviour. The reward will reinforce the calm behaviour and create a positive association.

Separation anxiety

The most powerful solution to treating dogs with separation anxiety is human company. This doesn't necessarily mean you, the owner, either. I have many clients that drop their dog off for doggy daycare at Pooches HQ and I can tell you those dogs are in the door without a backwards glance as their owner waits for that whimper goodbye and gets nothing but a wagging tail running off into the distance.

If you can't afford doggy daycare or a dog minder, then see if a neighbour, family or friend that works from home is happy to help out, or hire a dog walker to break up their day which can be more affordable than doggy daycare.

🐾 LET THEM INSIDE!

If you can't arrange human company, the next method to treating separation anxiety in dogs is to provide an environment in which the dog can relax when nobody is home. For many dogs this is achieved by simply having access to inside the house where they can snuggle in a spot that smells most of you.

🐾 CHANGE YOUR ROUTINE WHEN HEADING OUT

A way to help is to change your routine each day. Go out to your car with your keys and bag and come back in, sit down on the couch, turn the TV on and then head out again, only to come back inside again and do something else before quietly departing for the final time with little fuss. That way your dog doesn't get to know your every move and work themselves into a stressed state before you've even left them. If you pop back in and out, they can start to be desensitised to the departure a bit. This does take a lot of time and patience, but it is worth a try. Search for separation anxiety on poochesatplay.com to watch my video as to how this is done.

🐾 IMPLEMENT SOME INDEPENDENCE TRAINING

Talk to a dog trainer or vet about how you can start doing some independence training with your dog so that they are slowly re-introduced to spending more time alone, even when you are at home. This might be leaving them outside where they can still see you but occupied by a recreational bone (see pp. 70–71 for guidelines) or an interactive toy to work their brain and body.

DOGS LEARN OUR ROUTINE SO CHANGE IT REGULARLY BEFORE DEPARTING THE HOUSE

Refer to pp. 144–145 to where I talk about environmental enrichment to help ensure your dog has plenty to do when you are out, coupled with the independence training.

Thunderstorms and fireworks

Desensitising your dog to fireworks and thunderstorms as a puppy is the best way to ensure your dog will be unfazed by these noises later in life. However, for dogs that already have noise phobias it may take many weeks or months with the help of a professional to resolve the issue, if at all. So, to help here are some things you can do when you know it is going to be stormy or fireworks will be on.

🐾 SECURE IN A CRATE OR ROOM INSIDE THE HOUSE

If your dog is crate trained, then during a thunderstorm or fireworks display secure him in his crate with a chew toy or bone to occupy his time. If he's not crate trained, place his bed in a bedroom during the fireworks.

Find a room in the house (often the main bedroom is best as it also has a strong smell of you, particularly if you are not going to be at home) where the windows can be closed and put blinds down to help insulate them from seeing and hearing the storm. Place their dog bed or crate inside the room to help keep them sheltered with their usual blanket and favourite toy for comfort.

🐾 IF OUTSIDE – KEEP THEM SAFE

If you definitely can't leave them in the house during a thunderstorm or fireworks then make sure they have a protective kennel or area in the shed with a bed or blanket to keep them comfortable, warm and feeling protected.

If you don't have a shed, place their kennel close to the backdoor, under shelter and give them a bone or chew toy to keep them occupied, and ensure you escape-proof your yard. Dogs have been known to plunge from balconies, scale fences or burst through windows and walls when their fear is so great, so don't underestimate the threat.

❧ SOUNDPROOF THE AREA

Close all windows to the room they are being kept in, draw the curtains or blinds and play the radio or TV in that room and others in the house, to create a lot of white noise. Be mindful of the volume and what TV station it is on to avoid further frightening noises emitting from the TV.

❧ CREATE A POSITIVE ASSOCIATION

If you are at home with your dog during fireworks or a thunderstorm, particularly when you bring a new puppy home during their critical period then it is important to remain calm and relaxed, even if they think the world is caving in around them. We need to show them there is no danger, as they will be looking to us for reassurance. Darcy is sensitive to thunderstorms and fireworks but rather than make a fuss, I get out his favourite ball or squeaky toy and play games during the noise, to distract and counter-condition at the same time to help create a positive association with these sounds.

❧ PHEROMONE-BASED PRODUCTS AND HERBS

Pheromone-based collars, sprays and adapters you plug in the wall may also help some dogs with noise phobias.

❧ THUNDERSHIRTS

Some dogs respond well to the use of a Thundershirt, particularly if it is also combined with calming herbs or pheromone products. The theory behind these is that they wrap tightly around them like they are being held or being cuddled, which can help reassure them.

ARE YOU STRESSING OUT YOUR DOG?

In 2019, Scientists from Linköping University in Sweden found that the levels of stress in dogs and their owners mirror each other, so it is no wonder we are seeing a prevalence of stress and anxiety in our pet dogs.

Pet therapy has been found to be effective in reducing humans' stress levels but you need to be aware if you do suffer from anxiety that it may be affecting your dog as well.

Not only is taking time out and implementing strategies to reduce your own anxiety and stress levels important for your own mental and physical health, it is for our dogs too.

YOUR DOG AND WEATHER EXTREMES

Keeping your dog safe in summer

Our furry friends face many dangerous conditions over summer including heat stress, dehydration, snake and tick bites, sunburn and, especially in Australia, bushfires. However, by following some summer safety tips for pets, it can go a long way to help keep them safe.

TOP TEN SUMMER SAFETY TIPS

1. Always provide plenty of shade options, as the sun moves throughout the day, and cool, fresh water

2. Leave your dog where it is well-ventilated

3. Keep your dog out of the sun between 10am and 4pm

4. Check the heat of the footpath and road with your hands in the summer before walking your dog. If you can't leave your hand comfortably on the ground for 5 seconds, it is too hot for your dog's feet. It is best to walk early in the morning or when the sun goes down

5. Do NOT leave your pets in the car on warm days, even with windows down and in the shade. The temperature inside of a car can rise rapidly and dogs can't sweat like we do so they can overheat extremely quickly

6. If your dog is looking uncomfortably hot, cool them down with tap water (not iced). You can give them ice blocks to lick or in their water bowl

7. Use sunscreen on exposed noses and ears, and keep white dogs or those with bare bellies out of the sun

8. Keep them away from snake and tick prone areas, and get them to a vet if you suspect heat stroke, or a snake or tick bite as these can turn deadly very quickly!

9. Use tick treatments in high-risk areas at all times

10. If you live or holiday in an area prone to bushfires in summer make sure you have a bushfire evacuation plan for the whole family including your pets. This also applies to wildfire plans in fire-prone areas in other countries

Keeping your dog safe in winter

Cold winter snaps can be tough on our dogs, even here in Australia where our winters are much milder than other areas around the world where the cold conditions can be extremely harsh and dangerous to our furry friends.

Just as it is important to keep our pets safe from the heat, it is equally as important to keep them warm in the winter.

TEN TOP WINTER SAFETY TIPS

1. During storms and heavy rain, it is vital outdoor dogs can seek safe and secure shelter, protected from the elements and falling debris. Ideally, a safe area inside the home, or a warm and enclosed garage.

2. Dogs should have a sturdy kennel under shelter close to the house, as a minimum, with warm blankets and away from any draughts. Large enough for them to stand up in and turn around with 10 cm (4 in) of extra height and width.

3. Ensure they can't use anything to scale fences and there are no gaps in fencing, particularly if they are prone to anxiety, thunderstorm or noise phobias. *See* pp. 204–205 for more tips on dealing with dogs with thunderstorm phobia.

4. Dogs still need regular walks even in winter. Make sure they are kept warm in a coat, especially if you have a fine-coated dog, such as a greyhound or Staffordshire terrier. You can supplement short walks with games and exercise you can do together inside; obedience training, games of tug or chasing a ball, or even a game of hide and seek are a great idea.

5. Do not allow your dog to walk on stretches of frozen water as it may not be secure.

6. Check your dog's paws and dry them thoroughly after they've been outside as snow can compact between the toes of dogs with long hair.

7. Where snow and ice is prevalent then training them to wear booties can help protect their paws.

8. Using paw balm can also help to protect your dog's paws keeping them soft and supple during the cold months.

9. Dry off wet and muddy dogs after walks. If your dog is prone to matted hair, it is important to give them a comb or brush as the wet can make matting even worse, painfully pulling their skin and causing bacteria to form. *See* pp. 212–215 for grooming tips to help stop matting hair.

10. Open crackling fires can lead to singed fur or tails, so install a fireguard screen around fireplaces to eliminate burning and keep your pet away from hot ash and harmful fire-starter toxins. Also keep your pooch clear of portable heaters and cords, particularly from large, bouncy or boisterous dogs and wagging tails.

BRRRRRRR.....

GROOMING

Regular grooming helps to keep your dog's skin healthy and provides their coat with a protective barrier. It also helps to keep their hair free of matts which can be painful and cause infection. To help, I've compiled my top grooming tips for dogs of all breeds to keep them healthy from head to paw.

When to wash your dog – or not!
Washing your dog when he is dirty is not always the right thing to do. This may sound like strange advice, but if you have a dog with longer hair or a double coat and are not regularly brushing your dog or keeping up with regular professional grooms, their hair may be matted underneath. If this is the case and you wash them, you are going to make the matts much worse. This causes discomfort and pain to your dog's skin, and also dramatically increases the risk of bacteria and infection underneath.

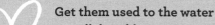

Get them used to the water
Not all dogs like water, so it is important not to force your dog into the bath or shower, or you will reinforce his fear. It is best to start getting him used to having a bath as early as possible when your dog is a puppy and making it a fun and positive experience. However, if you have an older or rescue dog that doesn't like having a bath, then you need to go back to basics and start by slowly reintroducing them to water again in a positive environment. Be careful not to reinforce their anxiety through your own behaviour. Having someone else to assist with holding a wriggling pooch or puppy may help, as may providing treats and positive reinforcement when they remain calm and starting very slowly one paw at a time.

Shampoo and conditioner

ALWAYS use pet shampoo and conditioner, never be tempted to use your shampoo or soap, as a dog's pH levels are very different to our own and could cause skin irritations or sensitivities.

You will also need to find a shampoo and conditioner that works best for your dog depending on their skin, coat or any allergies they may have. Just like I do for myself, I always use a 100% natural shampoo for dogs on Darcy to reduce any exposure to harmful and toxic chemicals.

Regular brushing at home

Regular brushing is vital to help keep your dog clean, prevent matting, increase circulation and reduce shedding. The amount of brushing your dog requires will depend on the length and type of coat. The rule of thumb is once a week, then an extra brush per week for every centimetre of hair length, i.e.: if your dog has hair that is 3cm (1½ in) long then you should be brushing it 3 times a week at home.

REGULAR BRUSHING CAN HELP BUILD YOUR BOND

How to care for a dog with a double coat

There are many common dog breeds that have a double coat including the german shepherd, pomeranian, chow, husky, malamute, corgi, border collie, any spitz breed and many more ... even the pug!

Regular brushing is a must, as is using a de-shedding brush or rake to remove the undercoat to help keep them cool in summer and avoid matted hair in the winter. Shaving a dog with a double coat is not the solution to keeping them cool in summer and can do more harm than good, so talk to a groomer about how you can best take care of your dog with a double coat. There are also some more tips on poochesatplay.com.

Professional groomers

Dogs with medium to long hair and dogs with curly hair need a regular visit to a professional groomer. Particularly breeds like poodles, poodle crosses, huskies, bichon frisé, maltese, pomeranians and similar, given they have quite specific hair grooming needs. Even if you are following our grooming tips for dogs here, a visit to a professional groomer from time to time can help keep a check on your dog's health as well.

Eyes

Regular trimming and cleaning of your dog's fringe and hair around its eyes is important. The hair near the eyes can collect a lot of dust and dirt, and, if it's not cleaned regularly, it can block the tear ducts and cause infection. It is also important to remove any gunk from around their eyes which can be as basic as using a damp cloth to gently clean the eye area.

Ears

Checking your dog's ears from time to time is very important. Some breeds are prone to getting ear infections so it's worthwhile knowing the symptoms of this. Symptoms can include scratching and rubbing at the ear(s) and head shaking. Take your dog to the vet if you see your dog displaying any of the symptoms above for longer than a day.

Nails

In nature, dogs' nails wear down naturally through contact with hard or rough surfaces. Today most dogs live mostly indoors and only walk for short distances. These pets may find that their nails need trimming as often as once a week.

SO, HOW DO YOU CUT YOUR DOG'S NAILS?

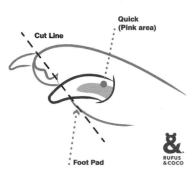

Quick (Pink area)

Cut Line

Foot Pad

RUFUS & COCO

Step 1: Start with just holding their paws and reward calm behaviour over a few days. Once they are okay with you touching their paws, you can move to the next step.

Step 2: You will need a good pair of stainless steel dog nail clippers with a safety guard to prevent you going too far, then start your dog off slowly. Start by just doing one nail, rewarding and letting your dog go. If all goes well, you can work your way up to a full set of nails at one time.

Step 3: Holding your dog's paw firmly (but not uncomfortably) in your hand, place the nail into the clippers, ensuring that the quick is not inside the cutting area.

Step 4: Angle the clippers at a 45-degree angle, as shown in the image above. This will remove most of the nail without cutting the quick. For dark nails, only trim 1–2mm at a time.

If you do accidentally cut too far, have some styptic powder or corn starch powder handy to quickly stop the bleeding.

The magic of massage

Just like exercise makes a dog feel good, massage can do wonders for your dog and is a great way to connect and share quality time together.

Darcy adores his morning ear rub in particular and it's no wonder. Dogs' ears contain a network of nerve branches that extend to internal organs, sending impulses throughout the body when you rub them. These help to relax your dog and even release feel good endorphins, so it's no wonder Darcy falls into a trance like state of bliss during his morning ritual.

To be able to give your dog a soothing ear massage, they obviously need to be comfortable with being touched. Start at the base of the ear, close to the head then firmly but gently rub the ear from the base to the tip and all around. I tend to focus on the inside of the ear with the back of the ear resting on my index finger and gently rubbing against that.

According to one of the pioneers in veterinary acupuncture and natural therapies in the USA, Dr Allen Schoen, acupressure massage can help if your pet has arthritis in a particular joint, if they have a stiff neck or back, and even if they have certain internal medical problems, by stimulating the body's own healing mechanisms in a similar way that reflexology has been used as an alternative medicine by humans for thousands of year.

Again, your dog has to be comfortable with being touched and not have any behavioural issues that might be triggered by you placing your hands on their face or body, particularly if they do have sore spots that they may react to. Darcy has some hip issues so I do have to be careful to not massage him to much or too hard around his hind quarters, as he will react and let me know if he is not happy. Remember when massaging or even patting your dog, watch their reactions and listen to what they may be trying to tell you.

In addition to helping foster a greater bond between you and your dog, massage may also be useful to help reduce anxiety and pain in certain conditions.

Stressful environments – Massage can help to reduce stress and anxiety during thunderstorms or fireworks, or any situation that makes your pet nervous and restless.

Arthritis – Gentle massage can increase circulation to sore muscles and joints. It is important not to press too hard, and stop if your pet flinches, moves away, nips or growls.

Before exercise – If your dog loves to run and chase, or is participating in dog sports, they may benefit from a gentle massage pre-exercise to stimulate circulation to increase blood supply to joints, muscles and nerves, which may help to prevent injury; much like massage works for a human athlete.

Post-activity – If your dog is anything like Darcy and his desire to chase the ball overrides any discomfort he might be in, resulting in him over-exerting himself, massage can help alleviate some of the stiffness and pain they might have afterwards.

TRAVEL WITH DOGS

I've compiled some of my top tips for ensuring your holiday is a safe and enjoyable one for the whole family, including your furry friends.

Do your research and plan ahead

- Call ahead well in advance and check on any rules and restrictions where you are planning to stay

- Look for dog-friendly places

Pre-departure preparations

- Vaccinations, and flea and tick treatments are up-to-date and relevant for the areas you are travelling to

- Take a copy of your vaccination certificate as you may need to show it before entry to parks and it is required for doggy daycare

- Identify local vets along your route or where you are travelling to

- Check your pet's microchip details are up-to-date and that they are wearing an ID tag with their name and your mobile number. *See* p. 181 for more information on this

WHAT TO PACK

- [ ] Leash & collar with ID tag
- [ ] Bed / blankets
- [ ] Travel or wire crate
- [ ] Favourite and interactive toys
- [ ] Food and water bowls
- [ ] Poo bags
- [ ] Wipes for mess
- [ ] Grooming tools – shampoo, towel, brush, nail clippers
- [ ] Toothbrush & dog-specific toothpaste for daily brushing
- [ ] Pet sunscreen / insect repellent
- [ ] Medications
- [ ] Pet first aid kit

BE PREPARED!

Car travel and anxiety

- 🐾 Only give them a light meal before the trip
- 🐾 Plenty of water
- 🐾 Stop every couple of hours for exercise and toilet and
- 🐾 Make sure the car is well ventilated or the window is down

If your pet suffers from motion sickness you might notice them looking listless or uneasy, licking their lips or drooling, or it can even develop into vomiting or diarrhoea. If you notice this, stop to let them walk around.

These signs and others, such as shaking or whining, might also indicate your pet has anxiety. If they do, it's important to go back to basics and get them used to car travel. Do this by taking slow, short and frequent trips and gradually increasing the length of the ride.

Take your dog to fun destinations (beach, dog park, etc.), to help create positive associations with car travel, reward them during and after each journey with small treats or praise for calm behaviour in the car. Taking along their favourite toy or blanket can also help, as can a calming spray or collar.

I have produced a free pet-friendly travel guide so you can visit poochesatplay.com to find out more or to download.

Air and sea travel

- Crate train your pet, or at least familiarise your pet well ahead of time with their travel crate and create a positive association with it. Check out poochesatplay.com for how to do this

- Only small meals prior to air and sea travel due to motion sickness risks

- Provide plenty of water prior to travel and ensure the airline or ferry provides water inside their crate so they can stay hydrated throughout their journey

- Avoid sedating your pet for travel as it can be harmful to them during the flight or ferry ride. It can lower their blood pressure and cause dehydration

- Calming collars or natural, oral, anti-stress alternatives for dogs provide another way to help pets feel as relaxed as possible during travel

- Ensure you know, and your dog is compliant, with any border security and other country specific regulations

- Another important factor is for owners to remain calm, so their pet doesn't pick up on their stress

CARING FOR OLDER DOGS

Here are some of my tips to help your ageing dog move into its senior years comfortably and with as much support as possible.

Dietary changes – It is important to change an ageing dog's diet to ensure they are getting the specific nutrients or extra supplements to help their joints, muscles and brain, such as Omega-3's (*see* p. 62).

Keep your dog's weight down – Keeping your dog at a healthy weight and physically active will help control arthritis and degenerative joint disease as he ages.

Twice yearly vet visits – Dogs are very good at hiding their pain, so once your dog gets to the age of six, twice yearly vet visits are recommended. In older pets it's very important to review weight, muscle tone, joint range of motion, diet, supplement protocol and exercise habits at least semi-annually, and so their nutritional needs can also be fine-tuned.

Start some alternative therapies – Regular massage can help keep your senior dog's muscles toned and reduce the slackening that comes with ageing. Massage also improves circulation, encourages lymphatic drainage, and eases joint stiffness as outlined on pp. 216–217. If your dog is in a lot of pain and has limited movement, talk to your vet about the physical therapy options that are available. Chiropractic adjustments, water exercises and acupuncture can also provide enormous benefits in keeping dogs mobile in their later years.

Don't stop the exercise – Senior and even geriatric dogs still need daily exercise to maintain good health and a resilient frame. While they may not be able to walk for as long or at the same intensity, it is still critical that they get regular walks and other age appropriate exercise to keep their bodies and minds active. Sticking to a predictable daily routine can help reduce anxiety and mental uncertainty, while treat release and food puzzle toys provide fun and mental stimulation.

Keep them comfortable – If they usually lay or sleep on the floor, consider introducing a bed or mattress, or switch to an orthopaedic mattress for larger dogs to help reduce pain in their joints.

A note about Dementia – Dogs with dementia will typically start to show symptoms by pacing at night, staring at the wall, getting stuck in corners of the room, vocalisation and potential indifference or a lack of recognition of their owners. Humans with dementia are usually quite content and so are pets in most cases. Just adjust their living area to have as few spots where they can get stuck as possible, keep their routine the same, take them on walks for some mental stimulation.

SAYING GOODBYE TO YOUR BELOVED PET

When I had to make the tough decision to euthanise my beloved Max, I wanted to make the best decision for him, not for me, by selfishly keeping him around too long because I needed him. He deteriorated quite quickly in a week so I made his last night as comfortable as possible, and laid with him in my arms in bed, gently holding him and letting him know how much I loved him. He looked ready to go and at peace when I carried him into the vets and held him throughout the entire process.

Euthanasia for your pet is a hard decision. Knowing when it is the right time is always difficult and many owners struggle with this decision but your vet can help.

Once you have said goodbye the grieving process begins, as it does when we lose any loved one. To help you, should you go through this in the future, here are some tips provided by an Australian company called Sweet Goodbye who help you care for your pet with dignity when they pass away with their home farewell and pet burial kits.

THINK ABOUT WHAT'S BEST FOR YOUR DOG'S NEEDS RATHER THAN YOUR OWN

AM I CRAZY TO HURT SO MUCH?

Intense grief over the loss of a pet is normal and natural. Don't let anyone tell you that it's silly, crazy or overly sentimental to grieve. Remember, you are not alone, thousands of pet owners have gone through the same feelings.

WHAT CAN I EXPECT TO FEEL?

Different people experience grief in different ways. Besides your sorrow and loss, you may also experience guilt, denial, anger and depression.

WHAT CAN I DO ABOUT MY FEELINGS?

The most important step you can take is to be honest about your feelings. Don't deny your pain, or your feelings of anger and guilt. Only by examining and coming to terms with your feelings can you begin to work through them. Express it.

WHO CAN I TALK TO?

If your family or friends love pets, they'll understand what you're going through. Don't hide your feelings in a misguided effort to appear strong and calm! Find someone you can talk to about how much your pet meant to you and how much you miss them – someone you feel comfortable crying and grieving with. If you don't have family or friends who understand, or if you need more help, look into support groups or ask your GP about grief counselling.

WHAT DO I DO NEXT?

When a pet dies, you must choose how to handle its remains. Sometimes, in the midst of grief, it may seem easiest to leave the pet at the clinic for disposal. To many, a pet cemetery provides a sense of dignity, security and permanence. Cremation can be an

YOU CAN FIND SOME MORE TIPS AT SWEETGOODBYE.COM.AU

affordable option that allows you to handle your pet's remains in a variety of ways: you can bury them, scatter them in a favourite location or keep them with you in a decorative urn. Consider your living situation, personal values, finances and future plans when making your decision. It's wise to make plans in advance, rather than hurriedly in the midst of grief.

WHAT SHOULD I TELL MY CHILDREN?

You are the best judge of how much information your children can handle about death and the loss of their pet. Don't underestimate them. You may find that, by being honest with them about your pet's death, you may be able to address some fears and misperceptions they have about death. Make it clear that your dog will not come back, but that he is happy and free of pain.

WILL MY OTHER PETS GRIEVE?

Your pets observe every change in your household and they are bound to notice the absence of a companion. Pets often form strong attachments to one another, and the survivor of such a pair may seem to grieve for its companion. Cats grieve for dogs, and dogs for cats. You may need to give your surviving pets a lot of extra attention and love to help them through this period. The love of your surviving pets can be wonderfully healing for your own grief.

SHOULD I GET A NEW PET RIGHT AWAY?

Generally, the answer is no. One needs time to work through grief and loss before attempting to build a relationship with a new pet. Children in particular may feel that loving a new pet is disloyal to the previous pet. A new pet should be acquired because you are ready to move forward and build a new relationship – rather than looking backward and mourning your loss.

WAITING FOR YOU

Saying goodbye is never easy to do,
especially to one so devoted to you.

From the moment you met love did abound,
life seems so empty when they're no longer around.

Raising a smile with their cute button nose, a wagging tail;
lifting sad spirits, they never fail.

As you shed tears for a friendship so true
take comfort their loving memory resides inside you.

Their body may be gone but their spirit is here,
in our hearts and minds they are always near.

When the time comes for your heart to stand still,
over the Rainbow Bridge, your friend waits on top of the hill.

Lara Shannon

SOURCES AND FURTHER READING

Useful websites

Pooches at Play, poochesatplay.com.au

Petfood Industry, petfoodindustry.com

PetMD, petmd.com

ASPCA, aspca.org

RSPCA UK, rspca.org.uk

RSPCA Australia, rspca.org.au

American Kennel Club, akc.org

Healthy Pets, healthypets.mercola.com

Banfield Pet Hospital, banfield.com

EAT

- Australian Veterinary Association (AVA), ava.com.au
- AgResearch Ltd NZ, agresearch.co.nz
- Massey University NZ, massey.ac.nz
- Liverpool University UK, WALTHAM™ Centre for Pet Nutrition, waltham.com
- American Association of Feed Control Officials (AAFCO), aafco.org
- Purina, purina.com
- Banfield Pet Hospital, banfield.com
- Hill's Science Diet, hillspet.com.au
- Royal Canin, royalcanin.com
- Big Dog Pet Foods, bigdogpetfoods.com
- PETstock Pty Ltd, petstock.com.au
- Pet Food Manufacturers' Association, pfma.org.uk
- Animal Medicines Australia, animalmedicinesaustralia.org.au
- *Pet Food in the US*, 14th Edition

- PetMD, petmd.com
  - 8 differences between dogs and wolves by P. Fitzsimmons, petmd.com/8-differences-between-dogs-and-wolves-0
  - 5 dos and don'ts when mixing your pet's food by A. Gallagher, petmd.com/blogs/thedailyvet/agallagher/2014/october/5-dos-and-donts-mixing-your-pets-food-32070
  - 5 common dog illnesses that are impacted by nutrition, petmd.com/dog/centers/nutrition/dog-diarrhea-and-other-diseases-impacted-by-nutrition
  - Food allergy myths (2011) petmd.com/blogs/nutritionnuggets/jcoates/2011/coates/food_allergy_myths-11862
  - What's in a balanced dog food? petmd.com/dog/nutrition/evr_dg_whats_in_a_balanced_dog_food
  - Carbohydrates: Key to a balanced dog food, petmd.com/dog/nutrition/evr_dg_carbohydrates_key_to_balanced_dog_food
  - What goes into making wet pet food? petmd.com/dog/nutrition/evr_multi_wet_pet_food
  - 5 dog nose facts you probably didn't know, by A. Semigran, petmd.com/dog/behavior/5-dog-nose-facts-you-probably-didnt-know
  - The importance of water for dog nutrition, petmd.com/dog/nutrition/evr_dg_the_importance_of_water
- RSPCA Australia, rspca.org.au
  - What should I feed my dog, kb.rspca.org.au/knowledge-base/what-should-i-feed-my-dog/
  - How is the pet food industry regulated in Australia? (April 2019) kb.rspca.org.au/knowledge-base/how-is-the-pet-food-industry-regulated-in-australia
- PFIAA (Pet Food Industry Association Australia), pfiaa.com.au
  - Cats, Dogs and Carbs pfiaa.com.au/feeding-pets/cats-dogs-and-carbs.aspx
  - Incidence, risk factors and managing obesity in dogs and cats, pfiaa.com.au/feeding-pets/Incidence-risk-factors-and-managing-obesity-in-dogs-and-cats.aspx
- American Kennel Club website, akc.org
- Australian Canine Cancer website, caninecancer.org.au
- CHOICE Australian consumer advocacy group, choice.com.au
  - Pet food regulation, (July 2018) by B. Bray, choice.com.au/outdoor/pets/products/articles/pet-food-regulation
  - Premium pet food, Does paying more for a supposedly higher quality pet food do you pet

any good? (July 2017) by K. Bray, choice.com.au/outdoor/pets/products/articles/premium-petfood-review
- Pet Food Institute, petfoodinstitute.org
  ○ Guaranteed analysis, petfoodinstitute.org/pet-food-matters/nutrition-2/guaranteed-analysis
- The Rawsome Effect, therawsomeeffect.com
- The Pet Food Institute, petfoodinstitute.org
- Association of American Feed Control Officials, aafco.org

PLAY

- Puppy Leaks, puppyleaks.com
  ○ The importance of play for dogs revealed, (December 2018) by J. Gabbard, puppyleaks.com/importance-play-dogs-revealed
- Companion Animal Psychology, companionanimalpsychology.com
  ○ Why do dogs play, (November 2017) by Z. Todd, companionanimalpsychology.com/2017/11/why-do-dogs-play.html
- *Genetics and the Social Behaviour of the Dog* by J.P. Scott and J.L. Fuller, The University of Chicago Press. Chicago (1965)
- *Handbook of Applied Dog Behaviour and Training – Volume 1 – Adaptation and Learning,* by S. Lindsay, Blackwell Publishing Company, Iowa (2000)
- *Handbook of Applied Dog Behaviour and Training – Volume 2 – Etiology and Assessment of Behaviour Problems,* by S. Lindsay, Blackwell Publishing Company, Iowa (2000)
- *Handbook of Applied Dog Behaviour and Training – Volume 3 – Procedures and Protocols* by S. Lindsay, Blackwell Publishing Company, Iowa (2005)

LOVE

- American Kennel Club, akc.org
  ○ How massage can help your dog by K. Fitzgerald, akc.org/expert-advice/health/massage-can-help-your-dog/
  ○ AKC's Chief Veterinary Officer Weighs In On Tick-Borne Diseases by J. Klein, akc.org/expert-advice/health/akcs-chief-veterinary-officer-on-tick-borne-disease-symptoms-prevention
- Banfield Pet Hospital, banfield.com
  ○ The Science Behind Skin Allergies, banfield.com/state-of-pet-health/skin-allergies/overview

- Longevity and mortality of owned dogs in England by C. O'Neill, D. Church, P. McCreevy, D. Brodbelt, P. Thomson, The Veterinary Journal 198(3):638-643 September 2013 DOI:10.1016/j.tvjl.2013.09.020
- American Society for the Prevention of Cruelty to Animals, aspca.org
  - Pet Statistics – Animal homelessness, shelter intake and surrender rates, aspca.org/animal-homelessness/shelter-intake-and-surrender/pet-statistics
  - How much will you spend on your dog in his lifetime by J. Reisen, akc.org/expert-advice/lifestyle/how-much-spend-on-dog-in-lifetime
- World Small Animal Veterinary Association, wsava.org
  - Guidelines for the vaccinations of dogs and cats by M.J. Day, M.C. Horzinek, R.D. Schultz, and R.A. Squires, wsava.org/WSAVA/media/documents/guidelines/WSAVA-vaccination-guidelines-2015.pdf
- Advantage Petcare, advantagepetcare.com.au
  - Flea allergy dermatitis in dogs and cats: Symptoms, treatment and prevention, advantagepetcare.com.au/au/parasites/fleas/flea-allergy-dermatitis-dogs-and-cats-symptoms-treatment-and-prevention
- VCA Hospitals, vcahospitals.com
  - Dental diseases in dogs by J. Bellows, vcahospitals.com/know-your-pet/dental-disease-in-dogs
- Pet MD, petmd.com
  - 5 scary consequences of neglecting your dog's teeth by P. Fitzsimmons, petmd.com/dog/general-health/5-scary-consequences-neglecting-your-dogs-teeth
- What's the Treatment for Cancer in Dogs? Is There a Cure? petmd.com/dog/conditions/cancer/what-do-when-your-dog-diagnosed-cancer-treatment-prognosis-and-aftercare
- Sweet Goodbye, sweetgoodbye.com.au
- Pet Positives, petpositives.com.au

INDEX

Photo credits

All images © Lara Shannon, except the following:
Front cover images iStock Images; p. iii, p. 3, p. 166, p. 207 Helen Black Photography; p. 10 @kaiserthegreyhound; p. 17 Big Dog Pet Foods; p. 18 @_ringo_unchained; p. 20 (top), p. 142 @axles_staffygram; p. 25 @absolute_kaos1; p. 47 @littlejerryboy; p. 128 Kerry Martin, Puppy Tales Photography; p. 148 @tassiejaxandralfofsydney; p. 175 Jamie Levy; p. 215 Rufus & Coco; p. viii, p. 55 (bottom), p. 57, p. 78, p. 87, p. 123, p. 153 Shutterstock; p. 5, p. 9, p. 14, p. 28, p. 36, p. 53, p. 60, p. 69, p. 103, p. 105, p. 106, p. 132, p. 134, p. 163, p. 170, p. 183, p. 194, p. 196, p. 211 iStock images; p. 16, p. 45, p. 46 The Noun Project; p. 21 (bottom) Unsplash/James Barker; p. 52, p. 66 Unsplash/Marek Szturc; p. 55 (top) Unsplash/Concha Mayo; p. 55 (middle) Unsplash/ Daniel Von Appen; p. 58 Unsplash/Zhaolong; p. 83 Unsplash/Lucian Dachman; p. 88, p. 90, p. 92, p. 93 The Rawsome Effect; p. 94 (left) Amanda McMahon; p. 94 (right) Willows Pantry; p. 96 Unsplash/Darinka Kievskaya; p. 104, p. 118, p. 119, p. 120, p. 122 Alamy; p. 131 Unsplash/Lenin Estrada; p. 140 Marvin Meyer/Unsplash; p. 157 Unsplash/Justin Veenema; p. 164 Unsplash/Adam Griffith; p. 179 Paje Victoria; p. 181 (top) Unsplash/Humphrey Muleba; p. 181 (middle) Unspalsh/Susan Matthiessen; p. 181 (bottom) Unsplash/Daniel Lincoln; p. 185 Unsplash/Daniel Maas; p. 186 Unsplash; p. 190 Unsplash; p. 208 Unsplash/Chloe Andrews; p. 214 Unsplash/Taylor; p. 216 Unsplash/Eric Ward; p. 227 Unsplash/Daniel Lincoln.

This book is dedicated to my dear friend Jean who would have been delighted to hear I had finally put pen to paper. Your friendship, constant encouragement and love for the 'doggies' is sorely missed but will never be forgotten.

About the author

A passionate animal welfare advocate and certified dog trainer and pet nutritionist, Lara Shannon has been a regular on Australian TV and radio stations for the past two decades promoting important animal conservation, dog training, behaviour and other pet care issues. In 2016, Lara created and is the producer and host of *Pooches at Play*, a lifestyle TV show to help entertain and educate people about how to care for and understand their dogs better, which airs on Australia's Network 10.

Lara is also the editor of poochesatplay.com, runs her own dog training and boarding business in Melbourne, Australia and is an ambassador for Second Chance Animal Rescue. She is dedicated to promoting responsible pet ownership and adoption through her endeavours to drastically reduce the number of dogs and cats that end up in pounds and shelters each year.

Never far from her side is the cheeky 'Dynamite Darcy', who Lara adopted in 2017, and has embraced his canine co-host position at *Pooches at Play* with great gusto!

Acknowledgements

The writing of this book is the culmination of many new beginnings, exciting adventures and, at times, overwhelming challenges to make the world a better place for our animals. Through it all I have been supported by so many people, it's impossible to thank you all individually – but to all of you – the family and friends, clients and organisations who have believed in me, provided words of advice and fuelled my passion for educating others about the issues close to my heart, I can't thank you enough.

Writing this book evolved from a desire to continue to spread the word about improving the lives of our furry friends, and without *Pooches at Play* and everyone who supported me in establishing my business and TV show, it would have been impossible.

Specifically I would like to thank my production partners David Byrne and Alex Begetis at The Rusty Cage, Richie Gee for your constant encouragement and publicist Adele Feletto.

Thanks to the amazing team at Hardie Grant Publishing for your support and enthusiasm to bring this book to life. Special thanks to Melissa Kayser, Megan Cuthbert and my editor Amanda McMahon who have made the process such an enjoyable experience.

I'd like to acknowledge the pet industry, dog training and health experts who have contributed to both my TV show and this book. In particular, Shane Young, Dion Collard and Michael Perna at PETstock. Special shout out to you Mick for taking the time to read through my first draft of EAT, which had enough information to produce an entire book about food and nutrition alone, so I know it was no easy feat!

Chris Essex at Big Dog Pet Foods and George Sleiman at the NDTF for believing in me and the concept for *Pooches at Play* from the very beginning, and helping to spread the word about the importance of good pet nutrition and dog training through your support.

Thank you to Kellie Johns at The Rawsome Effect and Andrea Lincke at Willows Pantry for sharing your recipes, and to Jean Flew, Georgia Simmons, Belinda Shipp, Jaime Levy, Steve Wiggins, Helen Black and Kerry Martin for your gorgeous photos. Also, Dr Kathy Cornack from Newcastle Holistic Vets, Nigel Wood from Ziwi Peak and Trish Harris from Four Paws K9 for sharing your knowledge freely with me.

Mum and Dad, who instilled the responsibility of owning a pet and how to love and care for them properly from when I was a toddler, you have always encouraged me to follow my dreams no matter what or where they take me, and I am blessed to have you as my parents.

Max, who was my special, temperamental little buddy, whose passing ignited the creation of *Pooches at Play,* and my cheeky sidekick 'Dynamite Darcy' who brings a smile to my face every day and never ceases to amaze me with his innate ability to find a well-hidden tennis ball or squeaky toy in the strangest of places.

To you, my reader and fellow dog lover, for taking the time to learn more about improving your dog's health and life in general. Every step we all take to improve the lives of our pets, is a step in the right direction to making the world a safer and more enjoyable place for our animals and for ourselves.

And last, but definitely not least, to every dog that has walked this earth. You enrich our lives, brighten our days and provide unconditional love and support.

Published in 2020 by Hardie Grant Travel, a division of
Hardie Grant Publishing

Hardie Grant Travel (Melbourne)
Building 1, 658 Church Street
Richmond, Victoria 3121
Hardie Grant Travel (Sydney)
Level 7, 45 Jones Street
Ultimo, NSW 2007

www.hardiegrant.com/au/travel

A catalogue record for this
book is available from the
National Library of Australia

Eat, Play, Love (Your Dog)
ISBN 9781741177053

10 9 8 7 6 5 4 3 2 1

Publisher
Melissa Kayser
Project editor
Megan Cuthbert
Editor
Amanda McMahon
Proofreader
Jessica Smith
Design
Hannah Janzen
Typesetting
Post Pre-press Group
Index
Max McMaster
Prepress
Post Pre-press Group and Splitting Image Colour Studio

Printed and bound in Singapore